WRITING ARABIC

WRITING ARABIC

A Practical Introduction to

Ruq'ah Script

by

T. F. MITCHELL

LECTURER IN LINGUISTICS
SCHOOL OF ORIENTAL AND AFRICAN STUDIES

GEOFFREY CUMBERLEGE
OXFORD UNIVERSITY PRESS
LONDON NEW YORK TORONTO
1953

Oxford University Press, Amen House, London E.C.4
GLASGOW NEW YORK TORONTO MELBOURNE WELLINGTON
BOMBAY CALCUTTA MADRAS KARACHI CAPE TOWN IBADAN
Geoffrey Cumberlege, Publisher to the University

PRINTED LITHOGRAPHICALLY IN GREAT BRITAIN
AT THE UNIVERSITY PRESS, OXFORD, BY
CHARLES BATEY, PRINTER TO THE UNIVERSITY

ACKNOWLEDGEMENTS

Professor J. R. Firth, Head of the Department of Phonetics and Linguistics at the School of Oriental and African Studies, has constantly emphasised the basic linguistic importance of the study of "letters". It is thanks to this stimulus, and to Professor Firth's counsel and encouragement in general, not to mention his handling of the difficult problem of publication, that the present book appears.

I should like also to acknowledge my indebtedness to Mr. T. H. O. Dawood, who taught me to write the Arabic Ruqɛah script. The credit for what is acceptable in my writing is due to the teacher: any imperfections are the pupil's.

As already mentioned, the book has presented a difficult publication problem; it has, for example, been necessary to type each page and subsequently fill in the examples before submission to the publishers for photographing page by page. My sincere thanks are due to Mrs. D. E. Newman for her extreme patience and excellent work on the typescript, to Mr. D. Cowan for his most careful revision and many helpful suggestions, and to the School of Oriental and African Studies for generously providing the funds to cover the whole cost of publication.

Finally, I wish to add my appreciation of the advice and technical assistance freely given by the publishers, the Oxford University Press.

T.F.M.

School of Oriental and African Studies,
1951.

Maestro. Que es gramática...?

Discípulo. El arte que enseña a conocer, unir, pronunciar y escribir [sic] rectamente y con propiedad las palabras.....

D. Torquato Torío de la Riva y Herrero
(Arte de Escribir)

INTRODUCTORY

1. This book was originally planned to appear in two parts, the first devoted to the written, and the second to the spoken form of Arabic. In the meantime, however, in collaboration with Professor J. R. Firth, I have re-written Gairdner's "Phonetics of Arabic" in which has been incorporated the material due to appear in the projected second part of the present book. The latter, therefore, is now concerned solely with the Arabic written symbol, but, to build his Arabic studies on firm foundations, the student should use both books, keeping in mind that the letter has not only shape but also phonetic power and grammatical function. He should study them serially in whichever order he pleases: it is felt inadvisable to use both simultaneously since systematic instruction in Arabic written and spoken forms must follow different sequences; thus, for example, when studying the written form, it is necessary to introduce ab initio letters the phonetic powers of which were best described at a later stage. Finally in this connection, both books should, of course, be studied in conjunction with a good grammar.

2. This little book is intended primarily to assist beginners. It is a curious fact that students of Arabic have in the past strangely neglected those elements of grammar without which there would be no grammar, viz. the letters. The infrequency with which one encounters European scholars having a knowledge of the Arabic script has often been observed, but we may go further and say that the number of those who write Arabic in an acceptable manner is remarkably small. We may note, too, in passing that handwriting shortcomings are not confined to students of languages having exotic scripts; a letter written in French by an English scholar of French rarely, if ever, <u>looks</u> French, and if the language had been, say, a Scandinavian one, the foreign origin of the writer would have been even more immediately revealed. There exists, then, it would seem, a definite hiatus at the beginning of all language instruction which a systematic study of

written forms would do much to remove. This hiatus is at its widest when the habitué of a given alphabet is confronted with another, when, for example, the user of a native roman script is called upon to write Arabic.

3. There is, too, an unjustifiable tendency among beginners either to look upon the Arabic script as something of a "bogey", or to consider its subsequent cultivation a waste of time once they have mastered what they consider to be the essentials. We can dispose of the first attitude with the assurance that the cult of the Arabic script is in no way esoteric, and that, given due application, its principles may be assimilated within a month. The second approach is probably inspired by a diffidence that is quite misplaced. Practice will soon produce a "good hand", and the advantages that this confers are surely patent. Apart from the need to cope with letters, manuscripts, etc., the sense of common courtesy demands that we strive to achieve at least a minimum of, not only phonetic, but also written acceptability. The ability to write (and pronounce) Arabic acceptably is a sure way of earning the Arab's respect; in this connection, it is well to remember that calligraphy among the many peoples who employ the Arabic alphabet is regarded as an art second only, if not equal to painting. There is a case in Arabic for the pen, and especially the reed-pen, being mightier than the sword.

4. The reed-pen is the essential tool of the calligrapher's art, with which he realises the pleasing "thicknesses" and "thinnesses" of his shapes. There is no mystery in how he achieves them: the truth is that if he obeys a few simple rules, he cannot help but achieve them. With care, patience and practice--and the greatest of these is practice--the student can attain a high standard of reed-pen calligraphy in a few months. The nib[1.] of the pen should be

1. The fashioning of the nib requires a sharp knife and a little care. If a competent native is available, then, if necessary, ask him to assist you in cutting your reed. After initial trimming, the nib

placed, and constantly maintained at an angle of approximately 60° (

): thereafter, whether it is desired to produce a curve or a straight line, provided that the writer moves the pen at all times in the appropriate direction in relation to the horizontal and/or the vertical, the correct shape will make itself. It is simply a question of practice and the ability to recognise whether a given shape is acceptable or otherwise. A good eye is as important to the writing of an unaccustomed alphabet as a good ear is to the speaking of a foreign language. The student should, therefore, in the early stages compare in every detail the shapes he produces with those which he knows to be acceptable, until at a later stage he comes instinctively to reject or accept his own shapes.

5. While reed-penmanship is a desirable end, it is realised that more everyday advantages are to be gained in learning to use and recognise running-hand forms, i.e. those forms made with, say, a fountain pen or an ordinary pencil in the normal course of writing. Analysis in the following chapters is based on reed-pen forms (henceforth termed "calligraphic"), but this gives rise to no difficulty since running-hand (henceforth "cursive") forms are, for the most part, directly relatable to their calligraphic counterparts. Where necessary, discrimination and explanatory remarks are made. Examples are given in both calligraphic and cursive form. It is not claimed that the examples achieve perfection in the rendering of the Arabic

---

(cont. from p.2)

should be cut slantwise at an angle which ensures that it is in contact with the paper along the whole of its length when the writer is holding the pen in the manner natural to him. Arab postures, including the method of gripping the pen and positioning the paper, usually differ from our own and there are, of course, individual variations, but I see no compelling reason for adopting a posture other than the writer's natural one. The nib should be as thin as possible consonant with durability. When trimming is complete, slit the reed lengthwise from the nib to ensure retention of ink.

This is how the finished nib should look:-

(See also Addendum on p.18)

script - far from it! - but at least they look Arabic and avoid the "howlers" which many Europeans and others have perpetrated for so long in the written form of the language. It is to be hoped that the student who aspires to a greater proficiency will eliminate any imperfections they now contain. In the early stages copy slavishly, down to the last detail, those forms which you know to be acceptable.

6. Calligraphers have devised and developed numerous styles of writing the Arabic script, each adapted to a given purpose. Thus, for example, Nasx is the printed form of Arabic; θuluθ is an ornamental style used for manuscript-illumination, mosque-decoration, etc.; Ruqεah, of Turkish origin, is the style known and used throughout the Arab world roughly east of Tripolitania, for the normal purposes of handwriting. There are numerous other styles but it is exclusively with Ruqεah that we shall concern ourselves in this book. The customary practice has been for the beginner to study and copy those shapes of the Arabic letters which appear in printed books, i.e. Nasx, but while Nasx is a perfectly legitimate object of calligraphic study, its forms have no place in a typical handwritten text of, say, Egypt, and will be of little help to the student who desires to cope with certain manuscripts, letters, etc. Moreover, in almost all cases, with the student left to his own devices, his efforts at reproducing acceptable Nasx forms fall woefully short. If he learns to write Ruqεah from the beginning, he will not find himself faced at a later stage with the distressing task of eradicating longstanding bad habits.

7. The book is concerned with essentials. Individual idiosyncrasies and variations are for the most part excluded, and may be collected by the student subsequently. They should not generally be imitated. Moreover, if Arabs at times do not clearly differentiate certain letters, that is no reason for us to imitate a bad example.

8. Discussion of the roman transcription employed lies without the scope of this book. Suffice it to say that a systematic tran-

scription of Classical Arabic is tantamount to a transliteration, while in devising the form of the present one account has been taken, inter alia, of the psychology of reading and writing, of the needs of cursive writing and the printer's requirements.

The symbols of the transcription appear on the following three pages. Where differences exist between them and those widely employed in transliterating Arabic, the transliterated forms have been included in brackets.

INTRODUCTION

1. The Arabic alphabet, which is written from right to left, consists of twenty-eight[1] letters; these are listed below in the order in which they are found in the dictionary.[2]

	CALLIGRAPHIC	CURSIVE	TRANSCRIPTION	NAME
1.	(ء) أ	(ء) ا	(i) ʕ (ʾ)	hamzah[3]
			(ii) aa(ā)	ʕalif(un)
2.	ب ب	ب ب	b	baaʕ(un)
3.	ت ت	ت ت	t	taaʕ(un)
4.	ث ث	ث ث	θ(th)	θaaʕ(un)
5.	ج	ج	j	jiim(un)
6.	ح	ح	ħ (ḥ)	ħaaʕ(un)
7.	خ	خ	x (kh)	xaaʕ(un)

1. See below: IX,2,B(i), Note.(c).

2. One current Arabic term for "alphabet", viz. الحروف الأبجدية [ʕal ħuruufu l ʕabjadiyatu] is an interesting anachronism. The second word is a mnemonic composed from the first four letters of an earlier order, viz. ʕalif, baaʕ, jiim, and daal. The modern order is largely a morphological one in which characters now having similar shapes have been juxtaposed as an aide-mémoire, the mnemonic remaining valid.

3. Hamzah (ء), really the first letter of the alphabet, has not been given separate treatment. It is dealt with under ʕalif, yaaʕ, and waaw, in turn.

	CALLIGRAPHIC	CURSIVE	TRANSCRIPTION	NAME
8.	د	د	d	daal(un)
9.	ذ	ذ	ð (dh)	ðaal(un)
10.	ر	ر	r	raaʔ(un)
11.	ز	ز	z	zaay(un)
12.	س	س	s	siin(un)
13.	ش سـ ـسـ ـس	ش سـ ـسـ ـس	ʃ (sh)	ʃiin(un)
14.	ص	ص	ʂ (ṣ)	ʂaad(un)
15.	ض صـ ـصـ ـص	ض صـ ـصـ ـص	ɖ (ḍ)	ɖaad(un)
16.	ط	ط	ʈ (ṭ)	ʈaaʔ(un)
17.	ظ	ظ	ð (ẓ)	ðaaʕ(un)
18.	ع	ع	ɛ (ʻ)	ɛayn(un)

	CALLIGRAPHIC	CURSIVE	TRANSCRIPTION	NAME
19.	غ	غ	ɣ (<u>gh</u>)	ɣayn(un)
20.	ف	ف	f	faaʕ(un)
21.	ق	ق	q	qaaf(un)
22.	ك	ك	k	kaaf(un)
23.	ل	ل	l	laam(un)
24.	م	م	m	miim(un)
25.	ن ن	ن ن	n	nuun(un)
26.	ه	ه	h	haaʕ(un)
27.	و	و	(i) w (ii) uu (ū)	waaw(un)
28.	ى	ى	(i) y (ii) ii (ī) (iii) aa (ā)	yaaʕ(un)

2. It is possible to divide the alphabet up or to make abstractions from it in many ways according to one's particular object of study. Thus Arab grammarians themselves have produced, for example,

(i) an historico-calligraphic division into "dotted" and "undotted" letters. It is often the presence or number of the dots that alone distinguishes one Arabic letter from another. Thus, for example, are differentiated:-

ز ر ; ذ د ; خ ح ج ; ث ت ب etc.

(ii) grammatico-phonetic divisions into:-

(a) "Weak" and "sound" letters. The so-called "weak" letters are ا , و , ى : the remainder are "sound". The significance of this classification is best discovered from a grammar book; it does not lie within the scope of the present volume.[1]

(b) "Sun" and "moon" letters. In junction with a following "sun" letter, the l of the definite article implies gemination of the "sun" letter. The "sun" letters are:-

ت, ث, د, ذ, ر, ز, س, ش, ص, ض, ط, ظ, ل, ن .

The remainder are the "moon" letters.

We may if we wish make a number of purely phonetic divisions and abstractions, or even evolve an entirely new phonetic order of the alphabet.

From the purely calligraphic point of view, however, there are two important alphabetical divisions. One we shall leave until later,[2]

1. The Arabic terms are ʕal ħuruufu l ṣiħaaħu and ʕal ħuruufu l juufu. In addition the old Arab grammarians distinguished between the "sound" letters and ħuruufu l jawfi or "chest" letters, the latter again being ا , و and ى. This differentiation appears to correspond to modern phonetic classification of consonants and vowels.

2. See III,2, below.

the other we must deal with immediately. It is the division into

"Separate" and "Inseparable" letters

Just as we join the letters of a word when writing English, so we must do for Arabic save in the case of six letters which, while joining a preceding "inseparable" letter, cannot be joined to a following letter. These six "separates" are:

ا , د , ذ , ر , ز , و .

Examples:-

فرس (= س + ر + ف), قوم (= م + و + قـ),

زوج (= ج + و + ز), أوقات (= ت + ا + قـ + و + أ).

The remaining letters are "inseparables".

3. For the purpose of writing, each inseparable letter may be said to have four forms. These are:

(i) Isolated

(ii) Initial

(iii) Medial

(iv) Final

This terminology refers, not to a word or a phonetic succession, but to a calligraphic group of letters. Thus, a letter which is final in a word in its written or spoken forms must have its "isolated" form--not its "final" form--when succeeding a "separate" letter. Again, a "separate" letter may be medial in the space-order or the phonetic succession of a word, but since it cannot join a following letter, it may have either its "isolated" or its "final" form in such a context, depending upon whether the preceding letter is a further "separate" or not. Calligraphically speaking, a "separate" letter cannot have either an initial or a medial form.[1]

4. Do not assume that a letter has only one, say, initial form. It would be truer to say that it has a characteristic contour in a

---

1. Thus the initial shape of an inseparable letter is that occurring either at the beginning of a word or in the "body" of a word after a "separate" provided that the "inseparable" is itself followed by at least one more letter.

given context, but that the contour may vary to a greater or lesser degree from context to context. Except, of course, in the case of the "separates", the shape of a letter is "controlled" principally by the shape of the following letter. This factor must include consideration of whether the following letter is medial or final. Thus, the shape of ب in the combination (final ى + ب)[1] is different from that in (medial ى + ب).[1] It follows that just as the shape of the initial letter in, for example, a three-letter word--all three letters being "inseparables"--depends upon the middle letter, so must the latter's shape depend on the final letter. Just as in speech, so in written Arabic the greatest profit is perhaps derived from study of the methods of joining the letter-isolates. Present-day emphasis on syntagmatic or "horizontal" study and analysis in phonetics and phonology, is equally justified in the treatment of written forms.

The fact is that the significant pattern is that of the word rather than the letter. That the word-contour as a whole may be said to be characteristic, is paralleled in the spoken form of Arabic words, and, moreover, reflects the usual three-radical framework of the language. The reader is directed towards a given meaning by the presence in the word of three radical consonants. Vowels are not among the foundations but are by way of being filled in by the initiated reader according to the context and the nature of the consonantal framework he sees before him on the page. One is reminded, by way of analogy, of the more popular and remunerative type of crossword puzzle. The introduction of vowel-notation is of relatively recent date, but, although the means exist, Arabic written texts are rarely "vowelled" ("pointed"). The method of notation, when resorted to, is one of diacritics, for the Arabic vowels, including zero-vowel,[2] are not letters (with the notable exception of the letters of prolongation, the sole concession the Arabs have deemed necessary to make to the reader[3]).

---

1. These terms should be read, of course, from right to left.

2. See 5(a) below.

3. And even these are simply adaptations of existing consonant shapes or the result of etymological change and analogy.

There has been no attempt to analyse syllables into consonants and vowels, an analysis so successfully completed by the Greeks and other non-Semitic users of an originally Semitic alphabet. In passing we may also note that in the West--down to the International Phonetic Association of the present day--we have been at pains to achieve a clear-cut differentiation of letters, while in Arabic the reverse process has evolved a number of fragmentary coalescent forms from letters originally quite distinct. Hence the dot-system of differentiating letters in Arabic, with its attendant loss of clarity. We must, however, remember that the Arabic script is syllabic and not in our sense alphabetic. The skeleton outline of the Arabic word, then, leads the reader to the right sphere of content, but thereafter it is up to him to supply, in the light of the context, the correct vowel-unit to each consonant. You can, in fact, read a text accurately only when you know the grammar.

5. The Notation of vowel-units and other diacritics.

(a) Vowel-units

It is necessary to recognise in Arabic distinction between three vowel-units only, viz. "fatḥah" [a], "kasrah" [i], and "ḍammah" [u]. The appropriate vowel-sign is placed over or under the consonant so vowelled in the spoken order of the word. The signs are as follows:-

fatḥah. A short diagonal stroke above the consonant.

kasrah. A short diagonal stroke beneath the consonant.

ḍammah. A small edition of و [waaw] above the consonant.

Examples: فَ [fa], بِ [bi], هُ [hu].

It is also necessary to distinguish in Classical Arabic between short and long varieties of the three vowels.

Long fatḥah. Usually, fatḥah followed by the ʕalif of prolongation[1] or, sometimes, yaaʕ.

e.g. رَا [raa], دَرَى [daraa].

---

1. See below I,2.

Long kasrah. kasrah followed by the "yaaʕ of prolongation."[1]

e.g. دِي [dii]

Long ḍammah. ḍammah followed by the "waaw of prolongation."[2]

e.g. ذُو [ðuu]

sukuun. The sign "sukuun" or "zero vowel", consisting of a small unclosed circle (ْ), may be placed above a consonant closing, or better, not opening a syllable.

It is sometimes stated--erroneously--that the Arabic letters are neutral as to vowels. On the contrary, the Arabic letter has syllabic value, that is to say it has inherent implication as to vowelling.[3] The Arabic letter should be interpreted (consonant + sonant), but since the sonant term has a twofold potential, a positive (a, i, u) and a zero (sukuun), the formula is better amended to (consonant ± sonant). Syllable-patterns are often differential in Arabic and sukuun is a prosodic device by which a syllable may be closed for patterning purposes. A letter having sukuun is said by the Arabs to be "resting," otherwise it is "moving". To develop a clearer view of sukuun's function by stating the negative corollary, we may say that a consonant having sukuun cannot open a syllable:[4] d, not r, may be said to close the

---

1. See below II,5(iii). 2. See below VIII,5(iii).

3. The Arabic word ħarf ("letter") would also seem to do duty for "syllable" in the writings of the Arab grammarians.

4. In certain other languages employing the Arabic script for their written form, "initial sukuun" is possible. Thus, in a recently modified form of writing Swahili, we find the initial groups مْب [mb-], نْغ [ŋ - English ng in "singer"], نْغ [ŋg - English ng in "finger"].

syllable in the word بُرْد [bard], but بَرْد differs from بَرَد [barad] largely because sukuun has been profitably employed to distinguish between a monosyllabic and a bisyllabic word.

This concept of a twofold contrast between a positive sonant and zero should be kept distinct from the threefold alternance of the vowel-system wherein the three positive vowel-units are mutually contrasting.

Note, finally, that the correct vowel-unit or zero is revealed when a given word appears in paradigm or in context.

(b) Other diacritics

Nunation.

The indefinite case-endings [un, an, in] of Classical Arabic are indicated by the device of doubling the appropriate vowel-sign. In the case of [an], ʕalif usually follows doubled fatħah.

e.g. ً (اً) [an], ٍ [in], ٌ (ٌ) [un]

taʃdiid.

When it is required to show that a consonant is to be pronounced double, the sign taʃdiid[1] (ّ) is placed above the consonant.

e.g. وَرَّدَ [warrada]

If kasrah or the termination [-in] follows a doubled consonant, the diacritic is placed above the letter but beneath taʃdiid.

e.g. رَبَّ = rabba, but رَبِّ = rabbi, رَبٍّ = rabbin.

1. Nowadays the term ʃaddah is widely used for the written symbol and taʃdiid for the feature of gemination.

maddah.

A sign, maddah, originally a horizontal ʕalif but now resembling a Spanish "tilde" in shape, is placed above ʕalif when a glottal stop followed by long fatħah is required in the pronunciation.

e.g. آ [ʕaa]

For the use of other diacritics, the student is referred to the grammar-books.

(c) The notation of "dots"

◆ = 1 dot;  = ◆◆ = 2 dots;  = ⁂ = 3 dots.

6. From the practical point of view, there are two possible approaches to the practical use of the book. One is to take all the forms of each letter in turn throughout the alphabet; alternatively, - and, it is considered, more desirably, - first to study the isolated shapes only of all the letters, and thereafter to proceed to their initial, medial, and final forms. Once the isolated shapes have been mastered, the rest is a comparatively simple matter for, firstly, in practising the complete art-figure isolate the student will be "getting his hand and eye in," and, secondly, it is in almost every case a salient feature (or salient features) of the isolated form that is used for the remaining forms. If the second method is adopted, it is suggested that the student should first use the table above (at the beginning of the Introduction) in conjunction with the individual sections below showing the isolated forms. Relative sizes of the letters may be seen in the concluding chapter,[1] where the letters are shown in relation to the line of writing.

7. The calligrapher's method of measuring the accuracy of his shapes by means of dots has been adopted, at least as far as the isolated calligraphic shapes are concerned. To draw a dot the nib of the reed-pen should be placed at 45° to the horizontal and drawn downwards and to the right--as shown in the diagram on p.17--until a perfect diamond has been produced.

1. XII.

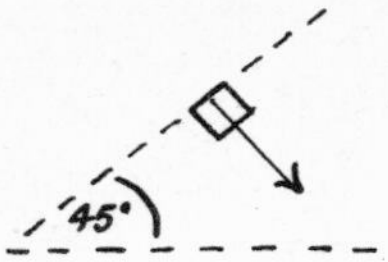

It is clear that the size of the dot, and therefore of the shape, must depend upon the width to which the nib has been cut.

8. The order of treatment of the letters follows the dictionary order as far as possible, but is based principally on calligraphic similarities existing between certain of them, even if such similarities are confined to one or two positions, i.e. initial, medial, etc. Thus, baaʕ (taaʕ, θaaʕ), nuun, and yaaʕ, though widely separated in the dictionary, are dealt with simultaneously since their initial and medial forms are differentiated by diacritics only.

9. The book is not to be considered a simple copy-book. Just as phonetics, so is an exotic script best studied within the framework of a language. This is an attempt to set forth a written system of Arabic within the framework of Classical Arabic words. The examples have necessarily been chosen--as far as existing words allow--with a view to exhausting all contextual possibilities. This has involved the introduction of letters out of turn, so to speak. Thus, for example, initial baaʕ will be found to have three possible shapes, the individual use of which depends upon the following letter. Initial baaʕ is therefore shown followed--in alphabetical order--by all the shapes before which it may occur, although most of them will not have been dealt with individually at this stage. At each section, therefore, the student should concentrate principally on the particular shape or shapes under consideration; he will find that, when he reaches haaʕ, all the pieces fit together. Thereafter, a second reading[1] should serve to confirm and, if necessary, complete the knowledge gained from the first.

1. Or use the ready-reference tables at Appendix D.

10. All the calligraphic examples are "pointed"; the student should, however, accustom himself in his further reading to the interpretation of the "unpointed" word. This necessarily involves study of the grammar-book. It will frequently be found that, abstracted from a "living" context, the isolated word-shape is capable of more than one interpretation; useful practice may be obtained collecting other vowel- and syllable-patterns to fit the word-shapes shown.[1]

11. We are primarily concerned in the book with the shapes of letters, but it must be remembered that a "letter" has not only shape but also name and function. Three letters, viz. ʕalif, waaw and yaaʕ, display a wide variety of functions. In a sense these functions are of the shapes themselves and must therefore be included, however summarily, in a book of this nature. Thus ʕalif, waaw and yaaʕ receive rather special treatment below. For more detailed accounts, refer to the grammar-book and dictionary.

Note: The cursive examples in the following chapters have been written rapidly without, as is evident, any conscious attempt at elegance. All examples are summarily translated at Appendix D.

ADDENDUM.

There is a general tendency to vary the width of the nib in accordance with the calligraphic style employed, especially when more than one style is used in a single context, e.g. advertisements, cigarette packets, etc. The following ascending order of width is recommended: (i) Nasx; (ii) Ruqεah, Diwaani; (iii) Persian (Nastaεliq); (iv) θuluθ. Differences of letter-size to be found in this book have been caused by the frequent need to refashion a new nib as the old one has worn down or broken. This lack of durability is a shortcoming of the reed-pen. For those who prefer metal, round hand pens (oblique reverse) in thirteen degrees of point (sc. sizes) may be obtained cheaply from suppliers of artists' and drawing office equipment or by writing direct to the makers.[2]

---

1. See, for example, II,3, Note (c) below.
2. British Pens Ltd., Pedigree Works, Bearwood Road, Birmingham.

I.

THE FUNCTIONS OF THE SHAPE ا [1]

There is some variation in the manner of naming the shape ا , and less uniformity still in the functions which it is called upon to fulfil. Its association with hamzah (ء) and the "innovation" of writing long fatḥah, have perhaps been the principle causes of confusion. The term (ا ± ء) is variously designated ʕalif hamzah or ʕalif, while, in turn, (ء ± ا) is either ʕalif hamzah or hamzah.[2] Moreover, the functions of the shape are many: thus, from a phonetic viewpoint alone, it may imply either consonantal or vocalic realisation. In short, hamzah (ء), ʕalif hamzah (أ or إ) and ʕalif (ا) have become intermingled to the extent of obscuring the fact that the first letter of the Arabic alphabet is really hamzah (sc. the glottal stop).[3]

Notwithstanding the uncertainty obtaining as to name and function, ʕalif is probably the most stable of the Arabic letters as to shape. The sign for hamzah, maddah, etc., may be written or not, but the vertical stroke is always present in a clearly recognisable form (except in the case of some archaisms - q.v. infra).

The most important functions of the shape ا are indicated below, but for a much fuller account the student is referred to the reference-books.[4] A similar variety of functions exists in the cases of the letters waaw (و) and yaaʕ (ى). A brief summary of their functions has therefore been included under their respective sections below.[5]

---

1. Note the slight forward slope of the shape.

2. Cf., say, the Indian Devanagari syllabary in which, under certain conditions, the names of the letters are equally their phonetic powers.

3. See also IX,2,B(i), Note.(c). 87/88

4. See, for example, Lane's Arabic Dictionary under ʕalif.

5. See II,5, and VIII,5.

1. <u>Bearer for hamzah:- أَلِفُ هَمْزَةٍ [ʕalifu hamzatin]</u>

(i) <u>hamzah in initial[1] and final[1] positions</u>.

In initial position, hamzah is always written with ʕalif, whatever the following vowel. If fatħah or ɖammah follows, hamzah is written above ʕalif; if kasrah follows, hamzah appears below.

In final position, after fatħah, hamzah is again always written with ʕalif, whatever the following vowel.

Examples:-

1. أَذِنَ	2. اِبْنٌ ← Hamzah Missing !!!	3. أُمٌّ
اُذِنَ	اِبن	اُم
ʕaðina.	ʕibnun.	ʕummun.
4. يَرْبَأُ	5. نَبَّأَ	6. يَنْشَأْ
يربأُ	نبأ	ينشأْ
yarbaʕu.	nabbaʕa.	yanʃaʕ.

(ii) <u>hamzah in medial[1] position</u>.

In medial position, ʕalif is used to support hamzah:-

a) after sukuun and before fatħah.[2]

b) after fatħah and before fatħah.

c) after fatħah and before sukuun.

---

1. These terms refer here to the position of the glottal stop in the phonetic form of a word. It will be found that with calligraphic reference the terms are used somewhat differently; the student must, when he meets them, interpret them in the light of the context.

2. Unless the ʕalif of prolongation--see 2 below--precedes, in which case hamzah is written independently.

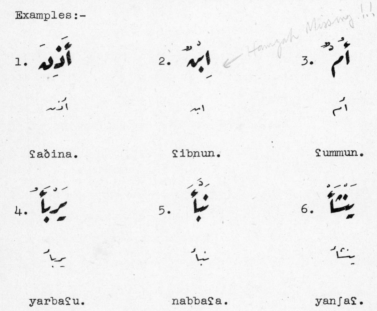

Examples:-

7. مَسْأَلَةٌ   8. يَسْأَلُ   9. سَأَلَ

   مسأله   يسأل   سأل

   masʕalatun.   yasʕalu.   saʕala.

10. اِمْرَأَةٌ   11. بَأْسٌ   12. يَأْنَسُ

    امرأه   بأس   يأنس

    ʕimraʕatun.   baʕsun.   yaʕnas.

(i) and (ii) above illustrate a consonantal function
of ʕalif, when, accompanied by hamzah (sc. ﺀ), it is
the written symbol for the glottal stop.

Note that the initial hamzah which is "suppressed" when
not initial[1] in a word-group (sc. hamzatu l waṣli) usually
appears in the writing in the form of ʕalif alone, i.e.
without ﺀ . This "suppressible" hamzah is rendered in
the spoken form of the word in isolation, or when initial
in a word-group or after pause, since it is a fundamental
principle of Classical Arabic phonology that every syllable must begin with a consonant.

As might be expected, there is considerable uncertainty
as to the method of writing hamzah. It is not suggested
that the rules formulated here and under the appropriate
sections of yaaʕ and waaw below[2] exhaust the possibilities,
but the devices indicated are, at least, the most usual
and acceptable, and are readily committed to memory.

---

1. In the phonetic sense.
2. See II,5(i) and VIII,5(i).

2. The ʕalif of prolongation:- اَلْأَلِفُ اللَّيِّنَةُ [ʕal ʕalifu l layyinatu] (lit. "the soft ʕalif").

This use of ʕalif is usually prosodic, the shape symbolising the prosody of vowel-length with its resultant implications as to syllabic quantity and the place of the prominent syllable in the word.

An etymological function of this ʕalif is to represent--in both the written and phonetic forms of a word--a radical waaw or yaaʕ. The Arabs have, for example, preferred writing اَ to writing وَ and stating a convention for pronunciation purposes. Thus, جَازَ [jaaza] < جَوَزَ [jawaza].

Phonetically and phonologically, this ʕalif is always to be interpreted as long fatħah (transcribed aa).

Examples:-

1. قَامَ	2. عَارٌ	3. مَارٌّ
قام	عار	مار
qaama.	ɛaarun.	maarrun.
4. شَابٌّ	5. سَارَ	6. جَاءَ
شاب	سار	جاء
ʃaabbun.	saara.	jaaʕa.

Note.

A final long vowel aa does not always appear in the shape ا. It is sometimes rendered by yaaʕ following fatħah, as, for example, in رَمَى [ramaa], عَلَى [ɛalaa], etc. This is the so-called "ʕalifun bi ṣuurati l yaaʕi" ("ʕalif in the shape of yaaʕ").[1] It should be observed

---

1. See II,5(iv).

that the yaaʕ of, for example, رَمَى (> رَمَيَ), although a radical in its own right, is replaced in the writing by ʕalif, when the vowel aa is no longer final; for example, رماه [ramaahu]. Attempts at rendering orthography phonetic lead so frequently to inconsistency.

It is of interest to note that the final aa vowel has its own individual name in Arabic, viz. ʕalifun maqṣuuratun ("reducible ʕalif"). This would seem to indicate that, at least nowadays, the name ʕalif is clearly associated with the phonetic function aa. The vowel is shortened to [a] before hamzatu l waṣli: hence the name.

<u>Other Miscellaneous Functions.</u>

(i) <u>"'Otiose' ʕalif"; أَلِفُ ٱلْجَمَاعَةِ [ʕalifu l jamaaεati]</u>

ʕalif is here simply a calligraphic device emphasising certain personal endings of the verb. (3 pl.m. Perfect, 2 and 3 pl.m. Imperfect Subjunctive and Jussive, 2 pl.m. Imperative).

Examples:-

1. كَتَبُوا

كتبوا

katabuu.

2. يَكْتُبُوا

يكتبوا

yaktubuu.

3. يَكُونُوا

يكونوا

yakuunuu.

4. اُكْتُبُوا ← HAMZAH OMITTED

اكتبوا

ʕuktubuu.

(ii) The termination -an; اَلتَّنْوِينُ مَعَ الفَتْحَةِ [ʕal tanwiinu maɛa l fatħati]

The termination -an, usually the accusative form of the so-called "nunation", is written اً except:-

a) after ة, the special written form of the feminine and unit-ending [taaʕun marbuuṭatun].[1]

b) after hamzah, following a "long fatħah" [ʕalif].

c) when an < ayun.

Examples:-

5. بَابًا	6. أَسَدًا	7. مَلِكًا
بابا	اسدا	ملكا
baaban.	ʕasadan.	malikan.
8. شَيْئًا		
شيئا		
ʃayʕan.[2]		

but:-

9. زَوْجَةً	10. جَزَاءً	11. هُدًى
زوجة	جزاء	هدى
zawjatan.	jazaaʕan.	hudan.

1. See XI,4.

2. See p.40, Note 1 , and VIII,5(i).

(iii) ʕalif with maddah (~).[1]

The phonetic implication of آ is invariably [ʕaa], i.e. the glottal stop followed by long fatħah. Maddah is thus sometimes a purely calligraphic device designed to obviate the writing of two successive (vertical) ʕalif's. It is, however, also used with phonetic and etymological as well as with calligraphic relevance when two hamzah's are potential in the same syllable, separated only by fatħah[2]; thus, for example, in Form IV of a verb the first radical of which is hamzah, أَأْ > آ [ʕaʕ > ʕaa]. The sequence ʕaʕC is inoperative in Arabic.

Examples:-

12. آمِنٌ

آمن

ʕaaminun.

13. رَآهُ

رآه

raʕaahu

14. تَآلَفَ

تآلف

taʕaalafa.

15. آلَفَ

آلف

ʕaalafa.

16. آلِفٌ

آلف

ʕaalifun.

---

1. This should be taken in conjunction with notes on hamzah elsewhere--under the functions of ا , و and ى. The glottal stop has this written form following fatħah or sukuun and before long fatħah.

2. This does not mean that two hamzah's may not occur consecutively in the written order of a word. If they do so occur, however, the second hamzah does not have sukuun but is the initial consonant of a new syllable, e.g. أَئِمَّةٌ (for آئِمَّةٌ , for أَأْمِمَةٌ) [ʕaʕimmatun].

(iv) Calligraphic archaisms: تَهْجِيَةٌ قَدِيمَةٌ [tahjiyatun qadiimatun] ("old spellings").

Examples:-

	17.	18.	19.
	حيٰوة	زكٰوة	توريٰة
	حيٰوة	زكٰوة	توريٰة
more usually:	حياة	زكاة	توراة
	ħayaatun.	zakaatun.	tawraatun.

also:-

20.	21.	22.
هٰذَا	ذٰلِكَ	لٰكِن
هذا	ذلك	لكن
haaðaa.	ðaalika.	laakin.

23.	24.
اَللّٰهُ	إِبْرٰهِيمُ
الله	إبراهيم
ʕallaahu.	ʕibraahiimu.

Note.

The forms having ـٰوة or ـٰية are properly archaisms in that they are no longer in current use. The other examples (all of common words) are still written as shown save that the short vertical stroke is omitted in most cases; thus the fact that هٰذا is to be rendered [haaðaa] must be committed to memory. On the other hand, the stroke is commonly retained in those personal names in which it occurs.

II.

baaʕ, taaʕ, θaaʕ; nuun; yaaʕ.

These five letters are treated simultaneously since their initial and medial forms are differentiated by dots only.

I. Isolated Forms.

baaʕ, taaʕ, θaaʕ   nuun   yaaʕ

Note: When using a reed-pen the student is advised, at least until he has achieved a reasonable fluency, to attempt the shapes bit by bit rather than to make them without lifting the pen from the paper.

2. Initial Forms.

In initial position, these five letters assume one of three shapes, depending on the following letter. In most cases the shape is obligatory, but before certain shapes the writer may choose between variants. The three shapes, disregarding small non-significant variations, are (i) ـ (ii) ﯾ (iii) ^ . They are employed before the letter-shapes of the alphabet as follows:-

(i) Before ا , ب (medial and final shapes), د , ر , ك (medial and final shapes), ل (medial and final shapes), ~/ص (medial and final shapes)[1], ه (final shape) [2].

1. Examples containing the medial form of (~) and (ص) are not given below since the shape is as for medial baaʕ/taaʕ/θaaʕ.

2. Here and in similar headings subsequently shapes are employed as a convenient "shorthand" for the letters' names. At the same time, dots are omitted. Thus, for example, in the list under reference the shape د does duty for both daal and ðaal, ر for both raaʕ and zaay, and so on. Variant letter-shapes are included as a principle and call for some interpretation: thus hereafter at (ii) the three shapes (continued overleaf)

Examples:-

1. بَابٌ — باب — baabun.
2. نَبَشَ — نبش — nabaʃa.
3. بَتَّ — بت — batta.
4. ثَدْيٌ — ثدي — θadyun.
5. بَرْدٌ — برد — bardun.
6. يَكُرُّ — يكر — yakurru.
7. بِكَ — بك — bika.
8. تِلْمِيذٌ — تلميذ — tilmiiðun.
9. بَلْ — بل — bal.
10. أَيْنَ — أين — ʕayna.
11. اِبْنٌ — ابن — ʕibnun.
12. بِهِ — به — bihi.
13. بِهِ — به — bihi.

(continuation of footnote 2, p.27)........................ ـس ـسـ سـ س (m. and f.) must be understood as medial and final s/ʃ (differentiated only by dots) as well as any variant of final ʃ. Similarly for ṣ/ḍ indicated ـص ـصـ صـ ص (m. and f.).

Note.

The slight initial curvature of the shape before final nuun (Examples 10 and 11) is not essential, but is <u>de rigueur</u> before the first variety of final haaʕ (Example 12).
? NUUN

(ii) Before ا, ـس / ـسـ / ـسـ (m. and f.),[1] ص / صـ / ص (m. and f.),[1] ط (m. and f.), ع (m. and f.), ف (m. and f.), ـه (m. and f.), ق (m. and f.), ل (m. and f.), ـد, ى (f.).

Examples:-

14. نَابٌ	15. نَشِبَ	16. يَأْنَسُ
ناب	نشب	يأنس
naabun.	naʃiba.	yaʕnasu.
17. بَصَمَ	18. بَضَّ	19. بَطَّلَ
بصم	بض	بطل
baṣama.	baḍḍa.	baṭṭala.
20. رَابِطٌ	21. بَعَثَ	22. تَرَيَّعَ
رابط	بعث	تريع
raabiṭun.	baεaθa.	tarayyaεa.
23. يَفِدُ	24. زَنِفَ	25. نَقْدٌ
يفد	زنف	نقد
yafidu.	zanifa.	naqdun.

1. See note 2, p.27.

26. بَقٌّ

بق

baqqun.

27. يَكُرُّ

يكر

yakurru.

28. بِكَ

بك

bika.

29. تِلْمِيذٌ

تلميذ

tilmiiðun.

30. بَلْ

بل

bal.

31. ثَوْرٌ

ثور

θawrun.

32. بِي

.. بي

bii.

(iii) Before ح (m. and f.), م (m. and f.), ه (medial),[1] [~ (final)].[2]

Examples:-

33. تَحْتَ

تحت

tahta.

34. نَابِحٌ

نابح

naabihun.

35. ثَمَرٌ

ثمر

θamarun.

---

1. Form (ii). Vide infra XI,3.

2. See General Note (c) below.

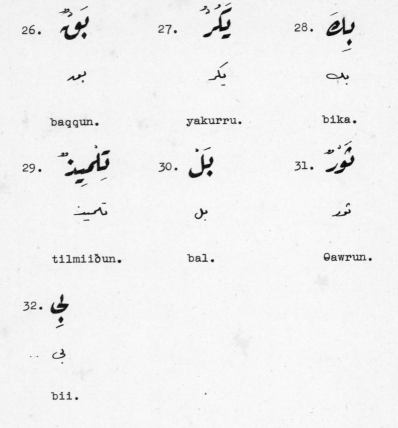

36. 

tamma.

37. 

nahrun.

38. 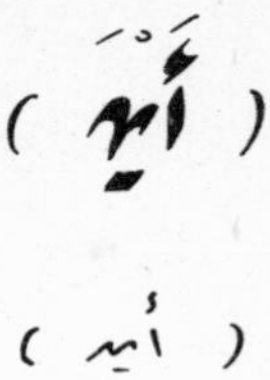

[ʕayna]

General Notes on the Initial Forms.

(a) Shapes (i) and (ii) are alternative before those shapes having a long vertical stroke, viz. ʕalif, kaaf, and laam. Of the two, however, (i) is commoner, and is therefore to be preferred.

(b) There are three variants of the shape before final nuun. Two are shown at Examples 10 (also 11) and 38. The third is as for Example 10 without the initial curvature, but is not shown.

(c) Example 38 is bracketed since, in calligraphic form, this variant of final nuun, dictating the shape of preceding b, t, θ, etc., is rare. It is, however, the usual cursive form (compare the calligraphic and cursive forms of Example 10). This V-shaped final nuun, while perfectly legitimate, is not adopted in the calligraphic forms given in this book; the curved contour of Example 10 has been preferred.

(d) There would seem to be a tendency, when writing "vertical" strokes, to rotate the nib towards the vertical in order to achieve a thinner stroke than would be possible with the "regulation" angle. This applies generally, for example, to form (ii) of the present shape.

(e) The shape in conjunction with final yaaʕ (Example 32) is rather specially contrived. The pen is usually removed from the paper after completion of the almost vertical downstroke, thus avoiding  or  , both of which are unacceptable. The latter is possible, however, in cursive form.

(f) It should, of course, be understood that the relevant form, viz. (ii), should be employed before <u>all</u> varieties of final ʃiin and ḍaad.

3. <u>Medial Forms.</u>

The medial form is, in almost all cases, initial form (i), the onset of the stroke appearing as a "tooth" above the level of the surrounding joining lines. The "bend-back" required by the letters jiim, ħaaʕ, xaaʕ, miim and yaaʕ (final) would, however, tend to fuse with the preceding joining-line, so that before these letters, a "modified" shape of medial b (t, θ, n, y) is employed. It therefore seems likely that this "modified" shape is but a variant dictated by the following letter. The significant feature is the prominence above the level of the surrounding joining-lines, this prominence taking the form of a "tooth" or of a rounded "bridge" (قنطرة)--as the Arab calligraphers call it--as occasion demands. The direction (and consequently the shape) of the joining-line is also dictated by the shape of the letters themselves, and helps to produce the characteristic individual word-contours.

A third rather special medial form is that used when one of the five occurs between two of its "fellow" shapes, e.g. θ + <u>b</u> + t, b + <u>n</u> + t, b + <u>y</u> + t, etc. The shape is 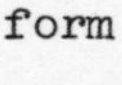 , in appearance a shortened variety of medial laam.[1] It should be noted that in such a succession of "like" shapes, even if they total more than three, it is the second one which takes this special form. Final nuun and yaaʕ are not, of course, included among these "like" shapes.

The distribution of the shape is, therefore, as follows:-

---

1. See IX,3,B(ii).

(i) Before medial and final ا , ـب , ـد , ـر , ـس , ـص , ـط , ـع , ـف , ـهـ , ـك , ـل , ـمـ , ـه , ـو ; and medial ـى .

Examples[1]:-

1. قَنَاةٌ	2. سَبَبٌ	3. يَبْدَأُ
قناة	سبب	يبدأ
qanaatun.	sababun.	yabdaʔu.
4. بِيرَةٌ	5. كَنَسَ	6. قَبَصَ
بيرة	كنس	قبص
biiratun.	kanasa.	qabaṣa.
7. اِسْتَنْظَفَ	8. تَبِعَ	9. حَنَّفَ
استنظف	تبع	حنف
ʔistanðafa.	tabiʕa.	ħannafa.
10. حَبَقَ	11. مُبَكِّرٌ	12. تَبَلَّلَ
حبق	مبكر	تبلل
ħabaqa.	mubakkirun.	taballala.

---

1. It is chiefly the final form of the following letter that is exemplified; the rule holds equally, however, before medial forms.

13. بَيَّنَ 14. سَنَةٌ 15. مَقْتُولٌ

بين سنة مقتول

bayyana. sanatun. maqtuulun.

(ii) Before medial and final ع and م , and final ى .

Examples:-

16. فَتَحَ 17. بَنَمَا 18. بَنَى

فتح بنما بنى

fataħa. banamaa. banaa.

(iii) "Special" context.

Examples:-

19. بَيْتٌ 20. مَنْبِتٌ 21. اِسْتِثْنَاءٌ

بيت منبت استثناء

baytun. manbitun. ʔistiΘnaaʔun.

22. يَتَبَيَّنَ

يتبين

yatabayyana.

<u>Notes</u>.

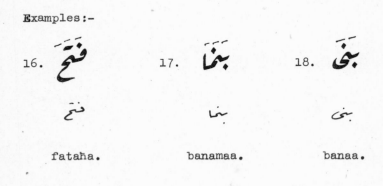

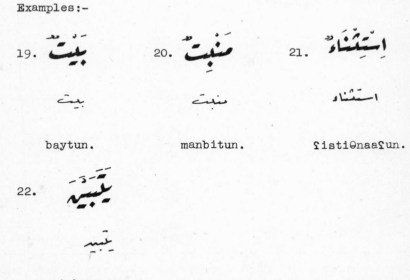

(a) The cursive form does not always agree with the calligraphic form. See, for instance, the combination b + y + r at Example 4; the "battlement" effect of medial b (t, θ, n, y) + r is usual in cursive writing. Compare, too, the fusion, in cursive form, of medial b, etc., with the usual form of final nuun. Thus, the dots are the surest means of distinguishing طن [ṭanna] and طين [ṭiinun]. See also Example 13.

(b) The method of joining letters is on the whole fairly uniform. The examples given in this book illustrate normal practice, but the possibility of other devices should not be overlooked. Thus, for example, بيت may equally be written بيت .

(c) The word-shape ٮٮٮ illustrates how important the dots have become for the ready interpretation of Arabic words in isolation. Its implications are many and include:

بيت	بنت	نبت	بيّت	ثبت	etc.
baytun.	bintun.	nabtun.	bayyata.	θabata.	

Sometimes, indeed, - as in the first and fourth examples - the dots are not enough, and in order to assure correct interpretation of the isolated shape, we must needs "point" it. Compare also, for example, بين [bayna] and بيّن [bayyana]. It is only when, knowing our grammar, we see the un-"pointed" shape in its place in the context, that we can interpret it immediately and accurately.

(d) The "bridge" shape of (ii) above is sometimes used as a variant only, after b (t, θ, n, y) before final nuun, e.g. بين [bayna].

(e) The "special" shape of (iii) above is not obligatory in cursive form but may always be preferred. ٮٮٮٮ , numerous "teeth" on the same level do not please.

(f) With further reference to (iii) above, do not use the "special" form for the second letter when the third "like" shape is of the "bridge" variety.

4. Final Forms.[1]

Generally speaking, it is the isolated form, <u>in toto</u> or minus the first stroke/s, that provides the final form of a letter. Some modification is made, however, in the case of final nuun derive from the isolated shape ں[2]; this does not apply to the ن shap of the letter.

Examples:-

(i) <u>b, t, θ</u>

1. حَنِثَ	2. حَجَبَ	3. نَسَبَ
حنث	حجب	نسب
ħaniθa.	ħajaba.	nasaba.
4. نَصَبَ	5. عَطَبٌ	6. لَعِبَ
نصب	عطب	لعب
naṣaba.	ʕaṭabun.	laʕiba.
7. لَقَبٌ	8. رَكِبَ	9. جَلَبَ
لقب	ركب	جلب
laqabun.	rakiba.	jalaba.

---

1. The student is reminded that "final" is used in its calligraphic sense. The final letter of a word will of course have its isolated form after a separate letter.

2. This shape has been preferred to ٮ --see above Note (c) on the initial forms.

10. سَمْتٌ　　11. لَهَثَ

سمت　　لهث

samtun.　　lahaθa.

(ii) n.

12. بَيْنَ　　13. نَحْنُ　　14. يُسِنُّ

بين　　نحن　　يسن

bayna.　　naħnu.　　yusinnu.

15. غُصْنٌ　　16. وَطَنٌ　　17. عَنْ

غصن　　وطن　　عن

ɣuṣnun.　　waṭanun.　　ɛan.

18. فَنٌّ　　19. كُنْ　　20. عَلَمٌ

فن　　كن　　علم

fannun.　　kun.　　ɛalanun.

21. أَمْنٌ　　22. هُنَّ

أمن　　هن

ʕamnun.　　hunna.

Notes.

(a) The junction of ṣaad with final nuun is marked by slight curvature; compare, for example, that of siin + final nuun, where the contour is quite sharply angled.

(b) Either of the other two varieties of nuun may, of course, be substituted above. Thus, for example, علن [ɛalanun] and هن [hunna]. The last shape is almost exclusively used for the cursive form; it is more sharply cornered than the shape used in the calligraphic examples above, which is generally more of a perfect "sine-wave" than the relevant portions of the isolated shape from which it derives (sc. ن).

(iii) y.

23. بِي	24. وَحْيٌ	25. نَسِيَ
بى	وحى	نسى
bii.	waħyun.	nasiya.
26. وَصِيٌّ	27. طَيٌّ	28. عِيٌّ
وصى	طى	عى
waṣiyyun.	ṭayyun.	ɛiyyun.
29. فِي	30. مَلَكِيٌّ	31. عَلِيٌّ
فى	ملكى	على
fii.	malikiyyun.	ɛaliyyun.

32. أُمِّيٌّ 33. هِيَ 34. نَهْيٌ

أمي هي نهي

ʕummiyyun. hiya. nahyun.

NB. There is a secondary form of final yaaʕ, rather more favoured in cursive than in calligraphic writing, especially when final in certain common particles. It is ـى ; for example, في [fii], على [ɛalaa], إلى [ʕilaa].

General Note on the Final Forms.

It will be seen that, variants apart, the final forms have one shape only, irrespective of the preceding letter. The shape of the joining-line from the preceding letter may change, but the significant final shapes-- ـب , ـم , ـى --are constant. This is true of the final forms of all letters. For this reason, it is not necessary to show every initial and medial shape after which the final form may occur. The above examples illustrate final forms preceded, in alphabetical succession, by the initial or medial form of the other letters of the alphabet. Dots are, of course, ignored as a general principle, and the appropriate form of the isolated shape ح does duty for jiim, ħaaʕ and xaaʕ, ط for ţaaʕ and ðaaʕ, and so on.

5. The Functions of yaaʕ-shape.

Like ʕalif, yaaʕ has a variety of functions. These are indicated in broad outline below.

(i) Bearer for hamzah: يَاءُ هَمْزَةٍ [yaaʕu hamzatin].

hamzah in medial and final position.

Broadly speaking, whenever kasrah precedes or follows hamzah, the latter is written above yaaʕ in medial or final form, as the case may be.

e.g. ـِئـَ ، ـُئِـ ، ـِئْ ، ـَئِـ

Examples:-

1. رَئِيسٌ[1]	2. رُئِيَ	3. بِئْرٌ
رئيس	رئى	بئر
raʕiisun.	ruʕiya.	biʕrun.
4. سُئِلَ	5. نَاشِئٌ	6. خَطِئَ
سئل	ناشئ	خطئ
suʕila.	naaʃiʕun.	xaṭiʕa.
7. نَائِمٌ		
نائم		
naaʕimun.		

(ii) Second Consonantal Function.

As we have seen, the Arabic alphabet consists of consonants only. Two of its members, yaaʕ and waaw,[2] are frequently realised in pronunciation as semi-vowels or as the final element

---

1. If hamzah precedes or follows yaaʕ of the long vowel [see section (iii) below], then a second yaaʕ-shape is necessary to carry it. Compare خطيئة [xaṭiiʕatun] (sometimes also written خطـئة, with hamzah written above a lengthened stroke joining yaaʕ to the following letter).

When yaaʕ-shape is used as hamzah's bearer, the two dots of its initial and medial forms are omitted, for the shape no longer symbolises the consonant-unit yaaʕ. A propos, the dots are regularly omitted in the final form of ى , whatever the function of its shape.

2. See below, VIII,5.

of diphthongs. Phonologically, however, they must be considered consonants in both these phonetic forms.[1]

"Semi-vocalic" yaaʕ [y] is always initial in a syllable. "Diphthongal" yaaʕ [ay] is always with sukuun, follows fatḥah and is either medial or final in a syllable. Doubling of the consonant--indicated in a "pointed" text by taʃdiid above it--sometimes implies a phonetic succession of "diphthongal" and "semi-vocalic" yaaʕ, but phonetically a geminated palatal fricative consonant is equally possible. Note that the succession "semi-vowel"-"diphthong" would require the writing of two separate yaaʕ's.

Examples:-

8. يَئِسَ

يئس

yaʕisa.

9. رُئِيَ

رئي

ruʕiya.

10. رَائِيَةٌ

رائية

raaʕiyatun.

11. بِيَعٌ

بيع

biyaεun.

12. بَيَّنَ

بين

bayyana.

13. أَيْنَ

أين

ʕayna.

14. بَيْتٌ

بيت

baytun.

---

1. The anaptyctic vowel used in Arabic and especially in the dialects to obviate, inter alia, the impossible pattern of three successive consonants at the same time reveals the true consonantal nature of

(continued overleaf)

(iii) The yaaʕ of prolongation: اليَاءُ اللَّيِّنَةُ [ʕal yaaʕu llayyinatu]

The second of the "matres lectionis" or "aids to reading", the first being the ʕalif of prolongation.[1] The symbols of prolongation are not strictly حُرُوفٌ [ħuruufun], a status which is reserved in the main for consonants only. They were originally considered unessential to the representation of the word--unessential, that is, to the grammarian or scholar. The Arabs have ever paid little heed to the problems of the normal reader, and it is conceivably this disregard of the reader's convenience that has rendered the Arabic script so unsuitable for combating illiteracy.

The yaaʕ of prolongation is long kasrah [ii]. It is written--in a "pointed" text--as kasrah followed by a yaaʕ which is medial or final in the syllable. Phonetically and phonologically, the yaaʕ of prolongation, when non-final in a word or word-group, must be followed by a consonant, either in the same syllable or beginning the next. It is necessary to understand this in order to be able to distinguish between "semi-vocalic" yaaʕ and the yaaʕ of prolongation, the first of which may, and the second of which must be preceded by kasrah; compare, for example, عِيَادَةٌ [ɛiyaadatun] and عِيسَى [ɛiisaa].

[yii] will require the writing of two separate yaaʕ's. "yaaʕ taʃdiid" [yy] preceded by kasrah has been interpreted throughout as a geminated consonant, i.e. not as long kasrah+ consonant yaaʕ. There is perhaps, however, a case for the latter interpretation in certain circumstances with a corresponding transcribed form [iiy]. Among other considerations, phonetic variants permit either interpretation.

(continued from p.41)

"diphthongal" yaaʕ. Thus, for example, the yaaʕ of the final "diphthongal" ay of the oblique dual form يَدَيْ [yaday] will in the construct before hamzatu l waṣl be provided with "anaptyptic kasrah" to "put it into motion"; فِي يَدَيِ الرَّجُلِ [fii yaday i l rajuli].

1. See above, I,2.

Examples:-

15. أَمِيرٌ   16. فَنَاجِينُ   17. رَئِيسٌ

أمير   فناجين   رئيس

ʕamiirun.   fanaajiinu.   raʕiisun.

18. فِلَسْطِينِيٌّ

فلسطيني

filasṭiiniyyun.

(iv) أَلِفٌ بِصُورَةِ الْيَاءِ [ʕalifun bi ṣuurati l yaaʕi][1]

For this term to be anything but a misnomer, we must again[2] consider the expression as having purely phonetic significance, viz. that it refers to the phonetic form [aa]. The shape ا must be excluded from its interpretation for, clearly, there is no question of yaaʕ replacing a true radical-shape ʕalif; moreover, developments of the order دَعَوَ > دَعَا, عَلِيوٌ > عَلِيٌّ , يَرْضَوَ > يَرْضَى have not given rise to such expressions as "waaw in the form of ʕalif" or "waaw in the form of yaaʕ". On the other hand, it is difficult, if not unjustifiable, to dissociate the shape ا from the name ʕalif. In this sense, the term is regrettable and, coupled with the introduction of ا when [aa] is no longer final (رمى but رماه), illustrates the fact that, even in Classical Arabic, attempts at keeping orthography in step with changing phonetic forms may sometimes lead to seemingly capricious results.

---

1. See also I,2, Note.
2. Idem.

Examples:-

19. بَنَى	20. عَلَى	21. إِلَى
بنى	على	إلى
banaa.	ɛalaa.	ʕilaa.

<u>Addendum</u>.

For yaaʕ in some archaic forms, see I,3(iv) above.

III.

jiim, ħaaʕ, xaaʕ.

1. Isolated Form.

Notes.

(a) The final "tail" of the shape is termed in Arabic ذَيْلٌ [ðaylun]. It is achieved by a final clockwise motion of the wrist, but the student, at least in the early stages, is recommended to draw the required shape in outline, and then "fill in".

(b) The enclosed upper part of the shape is termed [ṣunduuqun] ("box").

2. Initial Form.

The second calligraphic division of the alphabet[1] must be stated at this point. It is the division into الحُرُوفُ النَّازِلَةُ [ʕal ħuruufu l naazilatu] ("the descending letters") and الحُرُوفُ الصَّاعِدَةُ [ʕal ħuruufu l ṣaaɛidatu] ("the ascending letters). The shape of initial jiim, ħaaʕ and xaaʕ depends entirely on this classification; so largely do the initial and medial shapes of baaʕ, taaʕ, θaaʕ, nuun and yaaʕ.[2] The "ascending" letters are listed at (i), the "descending" at (ii) below.

1. See Introduction, paragraph 2.
2. See above II, 2 and 3.

(i) Before ا , ـب (m. and f.), ـد , ـس/ـسـ/سـ (m. and f.), ـص/ـصـ/صـ (m. and f.), ـط (m. and f.), ـع (m. and f.), ـف (m. and f.), ـهـ (m. and f.), ـك (m. and f.), ـل (m. and f.), ـنـ / ـن (m. and f.), ه (final--2nd form[1]), ـى (m.).

(حـ - ـحـ)

Examples:-

1. أَجَابَ	2. جُبْنٌ	3. جَدَّةٌ
أجاب	جبن	جدة
ʕajaaba.	jubnun.	jaddatun.
4. جِسْمٌ	5. حَصَلَ	6. حَطَبٌ
جسم	حصل	حطب
jismun.	ħaşala.	ħaţabun.
7. جَعَلَ	8. خَفَّ	9. حَقٌّ
جعل	خف	حق
jaεala.	xaffa.	ħaqqun.
10. حُكْمٌ	11. خِلَافٌ	12. حَنَّ
حكم	خلاف	حن
ħukmun.	xilaafun.	ħanna.

---

1. See above II,2(i), Example 13.

13. دَرَجَةٌ

درجة

darajatun.

(ii) Before ع (m. and f.), ر , م (m. and f.), ه (m.), ه (final - 1st form[1]), ى (f.).

(حـ - حـ)

Examples:-

14. حَجٌّ

حج

ħajjun.

15. جَرَى

جرى

jaraa.

16. خَمْسٌ

خمس

xamsun.

17. جَهِلَ

جهل

jahila.

18. دَرَجَةٌ

درجة

darajatun.

19. رُوحِيٌّ

روحي

ruuħiyyun.

Notes.

(a) The slight curvature before final haaʕ (1st form) illustrates the desire for curvature which is noticeable throughout Arab calligraphy; it is, however, less marked in Ruqʕah than in the other styles of writing.

(b) The first two strokes of medial form (ii) are as for the isolated form.

1. See above II,2(i), Example 12.

3. **Medial Form: (ـحـ - ـحـ).**

This shape is constant and is provided by stroke 2 of the isolated form. The "bend-back" beneath the preceding line is the significant feature, but, in cursive writing, is sometimes open to confusion with medial miim.[1] The stroke is not quite horizontal, and is identical with the second stroke of isolated yaaʕ.

Examples:-

1. مَحَا	2. نَحْبٌ	3. مَحَجٌّ
محا	نحب	محج
maħaa.	naħbun.	maħajjun.
4. نَجْدٌ	5. نَحْرٌ	6. يُحِسُّ
نجد	نحر	يحس
najdun.	naħrun.	yuħissu.
7. مَحْضٌ	8. سَخِطَ	9. نَجَعَ
محض	سخط	نجع
maħḍun.	saxiṭa.	najaɛa.
10. نَجَفٌ	11. مِحَكٌّ	12. مَحَلٌّ
نجف	محك	محل
najafun.	miħakkun.	maħallun.

1. See below X,3.

13. نَجْمٌ	14. نَحْنُ	15. مُخُّهُ
نجم	نحن	مخه
najmun.	naħnu.	muxxuhu.
16. نَحْوٌ	17. نَجِيٌّ	
نحو	نجي	
naħwun.	najiyyun.	

4. Final Form.

The final form is as for the medial form with the addition of the remainder of the isolated form.

Examples:-

1. نَابِحٌ	2. رَاجِحٌ	3. نَاسِجٌ
نابح	راجح	ناسج
naabiħun.	raajiħun.	naasijun.
4. نَاصِحٌ	5. نَاطِحٌ	6. نَافِحٌ
ناصح	ناطح	نافح
naaṣiħun.	naaṭiħun.	naafiħun.
7. كَحَّ	8. أَلَحَّ	9. سَامَحَ
كح	ألح	سامح
kaħħa.	ʕalaħħa.	saamaħa.

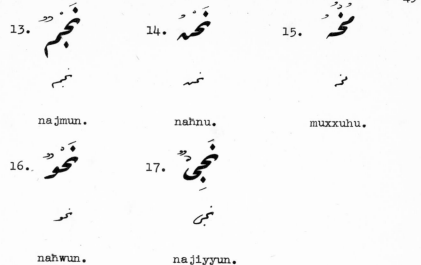

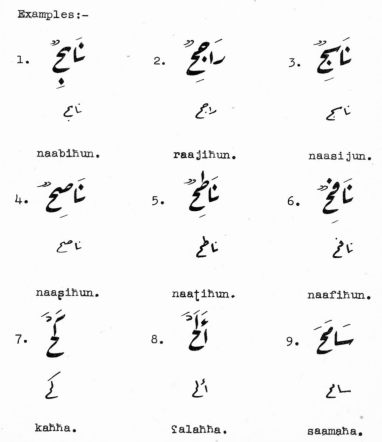

10. لَاهِجٌ

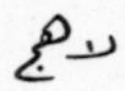

laahijun.

<u>Note</u>.

Initial kaaf and laam before final (and medial) jiim, ħaaʕ and xaaʕ[1] are formed--calligraphically--in the same way as initial baaʕ, taaʕ, θaaʕ, nuun and yaaʕ, before final yaaʕ, save that the vertical stroke is somewhat longer.[2]

---

1. Examples 7 and 8.
2. See II,2, Note (e).

IV.

daal, ðaal; raaʕ, zaay.

These four letters are all "separates". Therefore, calligraphically, they exist only in isolated or final form.

1. Isolated Forms.

daal, ðaal. raaʕ, zaay.

The shape of raaʕ, zaay, is possibly the most difficult to make with a reed-pen. The pen is drawn for a short distance in the direction of minimum thickness, then on a gradual curve before making a broad--not quite horizontal--sweep to the left. The student is advised to "touch up" at least the final part of the shape (dotted area in the dissected form above). To achieve the correct shape without "touching up", the "sweep" is "tailed off" by removing the lower half of the nib from the paper as you write. The straight-line effect of the lower edge of the shape is necessary (). The overall shape is roughly triangular ().

Examples:-

1. ذَهَبَ	2. أَدَبٌ	3. طَرَدَ
ذهب	أُدب	طرد
ðahaba.	ʕadabun.	ṭarada.
4. رَأَبَ	5. أَرْسَلَ	6. نُورٌ
رأب	أُرسل	نور
raʕaba.	ʕarsala.	nuurun.

2. Final Forms.

In final form, the two shapes (daal and ðaal) and (raaʕ and zaay) are distinguished only by the method of their being joined to the preceding letter. In the case of ـد an ascent, in the case of ـر a descent is made before the letter proper is made. For example, (b + d) is ـبد , but (b + r) ـبر .

Both shapes proper are with insignificant variations as for isolated raaʕ and zaay.

Examples:-

(i) daal, ðaal.

1. بَذَلَ	2. حَذَفَ	3. سَدِيمٌ
بذل	حذف	سديم
baðala.	ħaðafa.	sadiimun.
4. صَدَقَ	5. وَطَّدَ	6. عَذْبٌ
صدق	وطد	عذب
ṣadaqa.	waṭṭada.	ɛaðbun.
7. قَدِيمٌ	8. كَدَمَ	9. لَدْنٌ
قديم	كدم	لدن
qadiimun.	kadama.	ladnun.

10. مُذَكِّرَةٌ	11. هٰذَا
مذكرة	هذا
muðakkiratun.	haaðaa.

(ii) <u>raaʕ, zaay</u>

12. بَرَأَ	13. جَرَى	14. سَرَقَ
برأ	جرى	سرق
baraʕa.	jaraa.	saraqa.
15. صَرَفَ	16. طَرَدَ	17. عَزَّزَ
صرف	طرد	عزز
ṣarafa.	ṭarada.	ɛazzaza.
18. فَرَزَ	19. كَزٌّ	20. هَزَأَ
فرز	كز	هزأ
faraza.	kazzun.	hazaʕa.

<u>Notes</u>.

(a) In comparison with isolated raaʕ/zaay, there is a tendency for the "sweep" stroke to be made rather more horizontally in these final forms.

(b) Notice the "battlement" effect in cursive writing of the junction between raaʕ/zaay and preceding medial baaʕ, taaʕ, θaaʕ, nuun, yaaʕ,[1] as well as with preceding initial or medial ṣaad.[2]

1. See II,3(i), Example 4.
2. See Example 15 above.

V.

siin, ʃiin; ṣaad, ḍaad.

1. Isolated Forms.

A. siin ʃiin

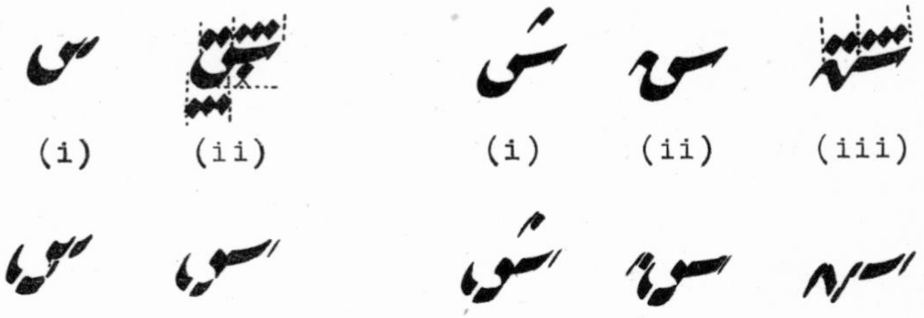

B. ṣaad ḍaad

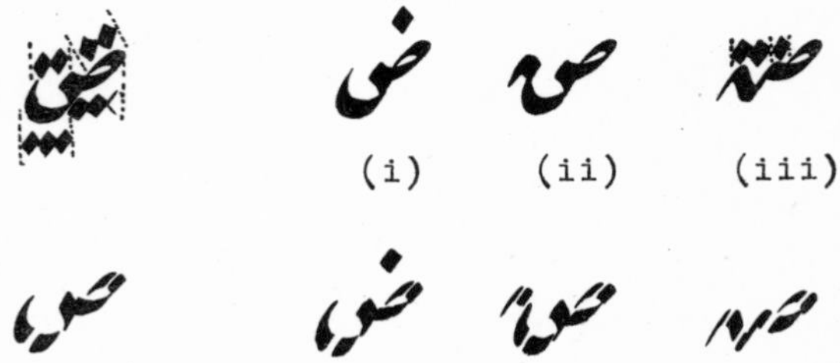

Notes.

(a) siin (i) is very rare in Ruqεah. It occurs most frequently in the initial form before ا , and in cursive form, virtually never.

(b) The last two strokes of form (ii) ʃiin and ḍaad are in place of the dot/s otherwise associated with the letters.

(c) ʃiin and ḍaad are capable of the variety of shape shown only in final position.

(d) In the case of all four letters--with the exception of form (iii) ʃiin and ḍaad--the ں-element is the same.

(e) The student may find the shapes difficult with a reed-pen. Remember to maintain the nib at a constant angle; thereafter, it is a question of acquiring the "feel" of the correct direction in which to move the pen. Movement is on a curve throughout.

(f) The enclosed part of ṣaad, ḍaad is--like that of jiim, ħaaʕ and xaaʕ--termed صُنْدُوقٌ [ṣunduuqun] ("box").

2. <u>Initial Forms.</u>

A. <u>siin, ʃiin</u>.

The long initial stroke of isolated siin/ʃiin is used to provide their initial (and medial) forms.

Examples:-

1. سَأَلَ (سَأَلَ)

سأل (سأل)

saʕala.

2. سَبَبٌ

سبب

sababun.

3. شَجَنٌ

شجن

ʃajanun.

4. سَدَنَ

سدن

sadana.

5. سَرَقَ

سرق

saraqa.

6. شِصٌّ

شص

ʃiṣṣun.

7. سَطْرٌ

سطر

saṭrun.

8. شِعَارٌ

شعار

ʃiɛaarun.

9. سَفَرٌ	10. شَكَّ	11. سَلَبَ
سفر	شك	سلب
safarun.	ʃakka.	salaba.
12. شَمَّ	13. شَهَادَةٌ	14. سُورٌ
شم	شهادة	سور
ʃamma.	ʃahaadatun.	suurun.

B. <u>ṣaad, ḍaad.</u>

(i) <u>Before all shapes except those at (ii) below. (صـ - صـ)</u>

Examples:-

15. صَابِرٌ	16. صَبَرَ	17. صَدَقَ
صابر	صبر	صدق
ṣaabirun.	ṣabara.	ṣadaqa.
18. ضَرَبَ	19. ضَعْفٌ	20. صَفٌّ
ضرب	ضعف	صف
ḍaraba.	ḍaɛfun.	ṣaffun.

21. ضَلَّ

ضل

ḍalla.

22. صِلَةٌ

صلة

ṣilatun.

23. صَهَرَ

صهر

ṣahara.

24. صَوَابٌ

صواب

ṣawaabun.

(ii) <u>Before ح (m. and f.), م (m. and f.), ى (f.)</u>

(صـ - صـ)

Examples:-

25. صَحِبَ

صحب

ṣaḥiba.

26. صَمَّمَ

صمم

ṣammama.

27. رَضِيَ

رضى

raḍiya.

<u>Notes</u>.

(a) The final stroke (ـ / ـ) of initial (and medial) ṣaad/ḍaad is thus a complete reflection of the first two medial forms of baaʕ, taaʕ, θaaʕ, nuun, yaaʕ.[1] A frequent practice in cursive writing, and one to be avoided, is the omission of this stroke in the initial and medial forms of ṣaad/ḍaad.

---

1. See above II,3(i) and (ii).

(b) Note the rather special cursive form of the junction with raaʕ/zaay.[1]

(c) Frequently, in the cursive form, the initial stroke of ṣaad/ḍaad remains below the "box".

3. Medial Forms.

A. siin, ʃiin.

1. تَشَاوَرَ	2. يُسَبِّبُ	3. يَسْحَبُ
تشاور	يسبب	يسحب
taʃaawara.	yusabbibu.	yasħabu.
4. حَسَدٌ	5. مَشْرُوعٌ	6. عَسَسٌ
حسد	مشروع	عسس
ħasadun.	maʃruuɛun.	ɛasasun.
7. يُسَطِّرُ	8. مَشْغُولٌ	9. يَسْفِرُ
يسطر	مشغول	يسفر
yusaṭṭiru.	maʃɣuulun.	yasfiru.
10. مُشْكِلَةٌ	11. يَسْلَمُ	12. اَلشَّمْسُ
مشكلة	يسلم	الشمس
muʃkilatun.	yaslamu.	ʕal ʃamsu.

1. See above IV,2, Note (b).

13. يُسِنُّ   14. مَشْهُورٌ   15. نَفْسُهُ

يسن   مشهور   نفسه

yusinnu.   maʃhuurun.   nafsuhu.

16. يَسُوءُ   17. نَسِيَ

يسوء   نسي

yasuuʕu.   nasiya.

B. ṣaad, ḍaad.

The distribution of the medial shape of ṣaad/ḍaad before the other letters of the alphabet is as for its initial shape.

In addition, the method of joining a preceding inseparable letter to medial (or final) ṣaad/ḍaad should be noted. The joining line is swept up and back to make the "box" of ṣaad/ḍaad, leaving a characteristic rounded corner below the "box". It is important that the lower edge of the "box", when completed, should be distinctly above the preceding joining-line.

(i) Before all shapes except those at (ii) below. (ـصـ - ـضـ)

Examples:-

18. حِصَانٌ   19. خَضَبَ   20. تَصَدَّرَ

حصان   خضب   تصدر

ħiṣaanun.   xaḍaba.   taṣaddara.

21. عَصَرَ

عصر

ɛaṣara.

22. لَصَّصَ

لصص

laṣṣaṣa.

23. مُصْطَنَعٌ

مصطنع

muṣṭanaɛun.

24. اِرْتَضَعَ

ارتضع

ʔirtaḍaɛa.

25. عُصْفُورٌ

عصفور

ɛuṣfuurun.

26. مِصَكٌّ

مصك

miṣakkun.

27. حَصَلَ

حصل

ħaṣala.

28. لَصَّصْنَ

لصصن

laṣṣaṣna.

29. مُصَهَّبٌ

مصهب

muṣahhabun.

30. فِضَّةٌ

فضة

fiḍḍatun.

31. خُصُومَةٌ

خصومة

xuṣuumatun.

(ii) <u>Before ع (m. and f.), م (m. and f.), ى (f.)(ـصى - ـضى)</u>

Examples:-

32. فَصُحَ

فصح

faṣuħa. (ɛ)

33. بَصَمَ

بصم

baṣama.

34. قَضَى

قضى

qaḍaa.

<u>Note</u>: It is important that the "box" of ṣaad/ḍaad should not be "blocked in".

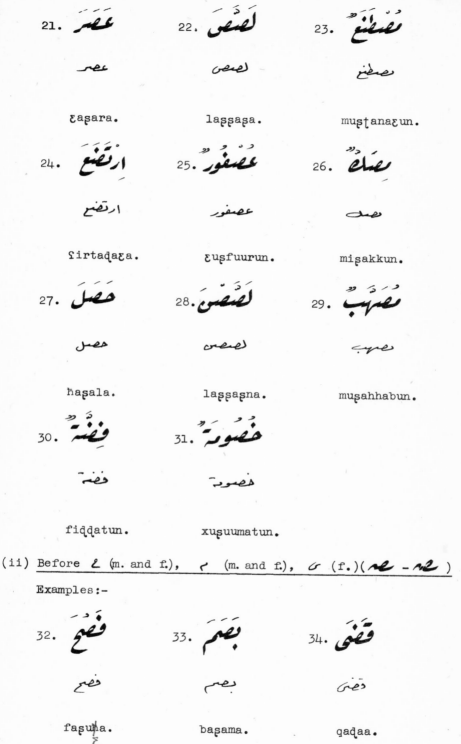

4. Final Forms.

A. siin, ʃiin.

Examples:-

1. رَأْسٌ

رأس

raʕsun.

2. جَيْشٌ

جيش

jayʃun.

3. بَخَسَ

بخس

baxasa.

4. عَسَسٌ

عسس

ɛasasun.

5. بَطَشَ

بطش

baṭaʃa.

6. غَشَّ

غش

ɣaʃʃa.

7. نَفَسٌ

نفس

nafasun.

8. نَقَشَ

نقش

naqaʃa.

9. نَكَسَ

نكس

nakasa.

10. رَمْسٌ

رمس

ramsun.

11. نَهَشَ

نهش

nahaʃa.

Notes.

(a) The shape سس may be either s + s or s + (b,t,θ,n,y) + s. The presence or absence of dots constitutes the sole means of differentiation. Compare, for example, حسس [ħassasa] and خسيس [xasiisun].

(b) Note the cursive distinction between s(ʃ) + m + s(ʃ) [سمس] and s(ʃ) + s(ʃ) [سس]. The letter is revealed by its relation to the surrounding joining-lines. Compare, for example, الشمس [ʕal ʃamsu] and عسس [ʕasasun].

(c) Ambiguity sometimes arises, especially in cursive writing. Thus ش may be either ʃ or (s + n). Similarly, (s + y) [سى] is often difficult to distinguish in cursive form from s [س].

B. <u>ṣaad, ḍaad.</u>

Examples:-

12. قَاضٍ	13. مَرِيضٌ	14. رَخِيصٌ
قاض	مريض	رخيص
qaaḍin.	mariiḍun.	raxiiṣun.
15. حَضَّ	16. لَصَّصَ	17. رَعَصَ
حض	لصص	رعص
ħaḍḍa.	laṣṣaṣa.	raɛaṣa.
18. بَعْضٌ	19. نَقَضَ	20. رَفَضَ
بعض	نقض	رفض
baɛḍun.	naqaḍa.	rafaḍa.

21. نَكَصَ

نكص

nakaṣa.

22. لِصٌّ

لص

liṣṣun.

23. مَصَّ

مص

maṣṣa.

24. أَرْهَصَ

ارهص

ʕarhaṣa.

VI.

ţaaʕ, ðaaʕ.

1. Isolated Form.

ط

Apart from the finishing stroke which is "tailed" (compare jiim, raaʕ, etc.), the lower half of ţaaʕ/ðaaʕ is as for the "box" of ṣaad/ḍaad. The final upright stroke is exactly as ʕalif; its lower extremity should not quite touch the "box".

2. Initial Form.

Examples:-

1. طَاهِرٌ	2. ظَبْيٌ	3. طَحَنَ
طاهر	ظبي	طحن
ţaahirun.	ðabyun.	ţaħana.
4. وَطَّدَ	5. ظَرْفٌ	6. طَسَلَ
وطد	ظرف	طسل
waţţada.	ðarfun.	ţasala.

7. طَعَنَ	8. طَفَحَ	9. ظَلَّ
طعن	طفح	ظل
ṭaεana.	ṭafaħa.	δalla.
10. طَمِعَ	11. ظَنَّ	12. ظَهَرَ
طمع	ظن	ظهر
ṭamiεa.	δanna.	δahara.
13. طَوْعًا		
طوعا		
ṭawεan.		

3. Medial Form: (ـطـ - ـط)

The characteristic shape of the preceding joining-line - exactly like that preceding ṣaad/ḍaad - is noteworthy. It occurs also, of course, before the final form.

Again as for ṣaad/ḍaad, the "box" is kept distinctly above the preceding joining-line.

Examples:-

1. خَطَأٌ	2. حَطَبٌ	3. بَطَحَ
خطأ	حطب	بطح
xaṭaʕun.	ħaṭabun.	baṭaħa.

4. مِيطَدَةٌ — ميطدة — miiţadatun.

5. نَظَرَ — نظر — naδara.

6. نُطْسٌ — نطس — nuţsun.

7. تَنَطَّعَ — تنطع — tanaţţaɛa.

8. مُطْفَأٌ — مطفأ — muţfaʕun.

9. نَطَقَ — نطق — naţaqa.

10. مَظْلُومٌ — مظلوم — maδluumun.

11. نَظَمَ — نظم — naδama.

12. حَفِظْنَ — حفظن — ħafiδna.

13. مُحَافَظَةٌ — محافظة — muħaafaδatun.

14. كَظُومًا — كظوما — kaδuuman.

15. نَفْطِيٌّ — نفطي — nafţiyyun.

4. Final Form.

Examples:-

1. رَبَطَ — ربط — rabaţa.

2. لَحْظٌ — لحظ — laħδun.

3. نَشِطَ — نشط — naʃiţa.

4. يَغُطُّ

يغط

yaɣuṭṭu.

5. حَفِظَ

حفظ

ħafiδa.

6. غَلِطَ

غلط

ɣaliṭa.

7. نَمَطٌ

نمط

namaṭun.

8. رَهْطٌ

رهط

rahṭun.

VII.

ɛayn, ɣayn.

i. Isolated Form.

ع

The lower part--the last two strokes (ے)--of the shape is as for that of jiim, ħaaʕ, xaaʕ.

It would appear likely that the phonetic similarities existing between ħaaʕ and ɛayn account for the likeness of shape. We may note in passing that the symbol for hamzah (ء) is derived from the upper part of ɛayn, its invention being attributed to the grammarian الخليل [ʕal xaliil], who considered its articulation as nearly approaching that of ɛayn.

2. Initial Form: (عـ - غـ)

Examples:-

1. غَائِبٌ	2. غَيْبٌ	3. عَجْزٌ
غائب	غيب	عجز
ɣaaʕibun.	ɣaybun.	ɛajzun.
4. عُذْرٌ	5. غَرَضٌ	6. عَسِمَ
عذر	غرض	عسم
ɛuðrun	ɣaraḍun.	ɛasima.

7. غَضَاضَةٌ	8. عَظْمٌ	9. عَقْلٌ
غضاضة	عظم	عقل
ɣadaadatun.	ɛaδmun.	ɛaqlun.
10. عَكْسٌ	11. غَلِطَ	12. عَمٌّ
عكس	غلط	عم
ɛaksun.	ɣaliṭa.	ɛammun.
13. عَنْ	14. عِهْنٌ	15. عَوْمٌ
عن	عهن	عوم
ɛan.	ɛihnun.	ɛawmun.

Note. In cursive writing an apparently gratuitous vertical stroke is sometimes used as the first stroke of the initial shape ( in place of ).

3. Medial Form.

To make medial (and the first part of final) ɛayn/ɣayn, the the reed-pen may be removed from the paper at the conclusion of the preceding joining-line, a suitable gap being left for the completion of the shape, which is made as follows:-

Stroke: (i) (ii) (iii)

Direction of movement:

The three strokes are, of course, fused in the complete form: 

Showing junction with preceding joining-line: (a) stroke (i) only: 
(b) complete shape: 

This procedure helps to avoid any tendency to obliterate or "over-round" the ^-shaped nick beneath the letter. ـعـ and ـعـ are unacceptable.

Examples:-

1. صِغَارٌ	2. بَعَثَ	3. مَعْنًى
صغار	بعث	معنى
ṣiɣaarun.	baɛaθa.	maɛnan.
4. نَعْجَةٌ	5. اِسْتَعَدَّ	6. يَغْرِسُ
نعجة	استعد	يغرس
naɛjatun.	ʔistaɛadda.	yaɣrisu.
7. اَلْغَشَّاشُ	8. يَغْضَبُ	9. يَعْظُمُ
الغشاش	يغضب	يعظم
ʔal ɣaʃʃaaʃu.	yaɣḍabu.	yaɛðumu.
10. شَغَفٌ	11. شُغْلٌ	12. لَغَمٌ
شغف	شغل	لغم
ʃaɣafun.	ʃuɣlun.	laɣamun.
13. لُغَةٌ	14. اَلْعَوْمُ	15. أَلْغَى
لغة	العوم	ألغى
luɣatun.	ʔal ɛawmu.	ʔalɣaa.

Note.

The shape should be "blocked" (ـعـ) not open (ـعـ) in order to avoid confusion with medial faaʕ and qaaf.[1] In practice, however, cursive medial ɣayn and faaʕ often become indistinguishable. In rapid writing the "unblocking" of ɛayn/ɣayn is often unavoidable, but an attempt should nevertheless be made to keep it flat-topped, and thus to distinguish it from the more rounded shape of medial faaʕ/qaaf.

4. Final Form.

The final calligraphic form requires the addition of the last two strokes of the isolated form to the first two strokes of the medial form.

Examples:-

1. بَلِيغٌ

بليغ

baliiɣun.

2. فَجَعَ

فجع

fajaɛa.

3. بَشِعٌ

بشع

baʃiɛun.

4. نَصَعَ

نصع

naṣaɛa.

5. سَطَعَ

سطع

saṭaɛa.

6. رَفَعَ

رفع

rafaɛa.

7. رَكَعَ

ركع

rakaɛa.

8. بَلَغَ

بلغ

balaɣa.

9. ثَمَغَ

ثمغ

θamaɣa.

1. See below VIII,3.

VIII.

faaʕ, qaaf; waaw.

1. Isolated Forms.

A. faaʕ | qaaf | waaw

The first two strokes of these three letters are, for practical purposes, identical: making . The "neck" (←) of waaw is normally somewhat shorter than that of faaʕ or qaaf.

The remainder of faaʕ is as for baaʕ/taaʕ/θaaʕ.

Thus: 

The remainder of qaaf consists principally of two strokes, the first gradually widening towards the bottom left hand corner of the shape, the second tapering vertically. In order to achieve this second stroke, it is thus necessary to modify the normal angle of the nib. The final "pennon" represents the two dots associated with the letter in its initial and medial forms, and in other styles of writing.

Thus: 

The remainder of waaw is as for raaʕ/zaay.

Thus: 

B. Examples of isolated waaw.

waaw is the last of the six "separate" letters.

1. 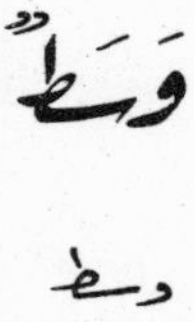

wasaṭun.

2. 

wardun.

3. 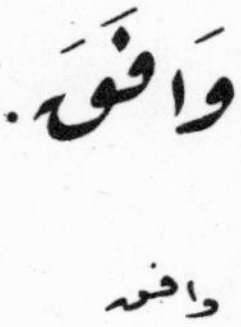

waafaqa.

4. وَقْتَمَا

وقتما

waqtamaa.

2. <u>Initial Form (faaʕ and qaaf): (فـ - قـ)</u>

faaʕ and qaaf are differentiated in their initial (and medial) form by their dots only.

Examples:-

1. فَاحَ	2. قَبَسَ	3. فَجْرٌ
فاح	قبس	فجر
faaħa.	qabasa.	fajrun.
4. قَدَّرَ	5. فَرَّ	6. قِسْمَةٌ
قدر	فر	قسمة
qaddara.	farra.	qismatun.
7. فَصَمَ	8. فَطِنَ	9. قَعَدَ
فصم	فطن	قعد
faṣama.	faṭina.	qaεada.
10. قَفَلَ	11. فَكَّرَ	12. قَلَمٌ
قفل	فكر	قلم
qafala.	fakkara.	qalamun.

13. قَمِينٌ 14. فَهْدٌ 15. وَقُودٌ

قمين فهد وقود

qamiinun. fahdun. waquudun.

Note: In cursive form initial faaʔ/qaaf often becomes difficult to distinguish in shape from initial miim.[1]

3. Medial Form (faaʔ and qaaf): (ـفـ - ـقـ)

The medial form of faaʔ/qaaf is an open loop, not unlike the "box" of ṣaad/ḍaad but smaller, and is distinguished from the "box" also by the fact that the preceding and following joining-lines are on the same level.

It is important that the loop of faaʔ/qaaf should be open, not blocked.

As already noted,[2] faaʔ/qaaf and ɛayn/ɣayn medial forms are often difficult to distinguish in cursive writing.

Examples:-

1. لِقَاءٌ 2. عَقَّبَ 3. نَفَحَ

لقاء عقب نفح

liqaaʔun. ɛaqqaba. nafaħa.

4. نَفِدَ 5. تَقْرِيرٌ 6. تَقَشَّعَ

نفد تقرير تقشع

nafidu. taqriirun. taqaʃʃaɛa.

---

1. See below X,2.
2. See above, VII,3, Note.

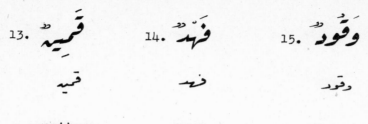

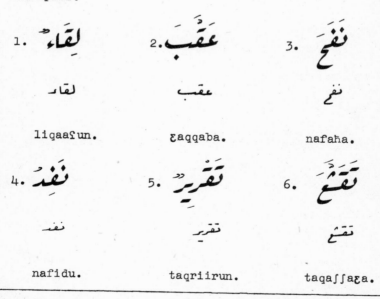

7. نَفَضَ	8. فَقَطْ	9. يَفْعَلُ
نفض	فقط	يفعل
nafaḍa.	faqaṭ.	yafεalu.
10. مُلَفَّفٌ	11. تَفَكَّرَ	12. اَلْقَمَرُ
ملفف	تفكر	القمر
mulaffafun.	tafakkara.	ʕal qamaru.
13. أَلِفْنَ	14. يَفْهَمُ	15. مُغْلَقَةٌ
ألفن	يفهم	مغلقة
ʕalifna	yafhamu.	muɣlaqatun.
16. مَغْفُورٌ	17. لَقِيَ	
مغفور	لقي	
maɣfuurun.	laqiya.	

4. Final Forms.

Final faaʕ and qaaf consist of the medial forms plus the last strokes of the isolated forms.

A. faaʕ.

Examples:-

1. شَرِيفٌ	2. رَجَفَ	3. عَسَفَ
شريف	رجف	عسف
ʃariifun.	raɟafa.	εasafa.

4. وَصَفَ	5. عَطَفَ	6. شَغَفَ
وصف	عطف	شغف
waṣafa.	ɛaṭafa.	ʃaɣafa.
7. وَقَفَ	8. وَكَفَ	9. حَلَفَ
وقف	وكف	حلف
waqafa.	wakafa.	ħalafa.
10. لَهِفَ		
لهف		
lahifa.		

B. <u>qaaf</u>.

Examples:-

11. عَبَقَ	12. سَحَقَ	13. وَسَقَ
عبق	سحق	وسق
ɛabaqa.	saħaqa.	wasaqa.
14. لَصِقَ	15. طَقَّ	16. صَعَقَ
لصق	طق	صعق
laṣiqa.	ṭaqqa.	ṣaɛaqa.

17. صَفَقَ

صفق

ṣafaqa.

18. عَلَّقَ

علق

ɛallaqa.

19. عَمُقَ

عمق

ɛamuqa.

20. رَهَقَ

رهق

rahaqa.

Note. In cursive script, final qaaf often resembles final nuun of the type ~ : the distinction between the two lies principally in the "head" of qaaf and in its greater curvature generally.

C. waaw: (و - ـو)

Examples:-

21. نُورٌ

نور

nuurun.

22. جَوَّدَ

جود

jawwada.

23. سِوَى

سوى

siwaa.

24. صَوْتٌ

صوت

ṣawtun.

25. طُولٌ

طول

ṭuulun.

26. مَشْغُولٌ

مشغول

maʃɣuulun.

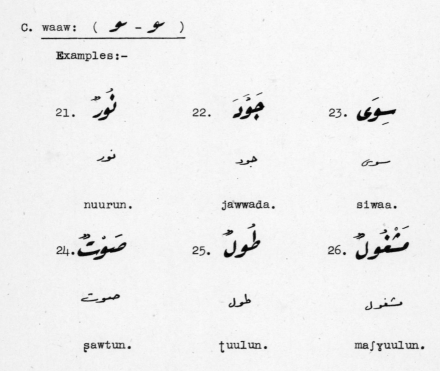

27. قَوْمٌ	28. لُوطٌ	29. مُوسِيقَى
قوم	لوط	موسيقى
qawmun.	luuṭun.	muusiiqaa.

5. <u>The Functions of waaw-shape.</u>

The following are the principal functions of the letter waaw:-

(i) <u>Bearer for hamzah in medial and final position:</u> وَاوُ هَمْزَةٍ <u>[waawu hamzatin]</u>.

Generally speaking, hamzah is written with waaw whenever ḍammah either precedes or follows, unless either of these positions is occupied by kasrah.[1]

Examples:-

1. بَؤُسَ	2. يُؤَلِّفُ	3. يَبْؤُسُ
بؤس	يؤلف	يبؤس
baʕusa.	yuʕallifu.	yabʕusu.
4. يُؤْخَذُ	5. دَنُؤَ	
يؤخذ	دنؤ	
yuʕxaðu.	danuʕa.	

<u>Concluding notes on hamzah</u>.

Some uncertainty exists when hamzah follows sukuun, witness

---

1. See above II,5(i).

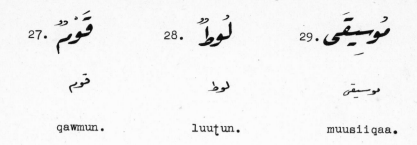

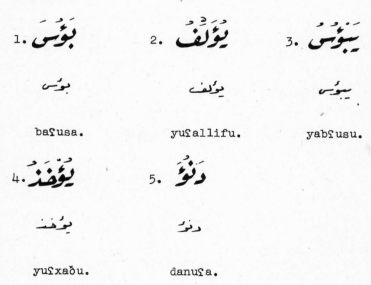

the variants مَسْؤُول and مَسْئُول [masʕuul].[1] This is perhaps in accord with the tacit implication in our examination of hamzah that neighbouring kasrah exerts the strongest "influence". The nature, i.e. "separate" or "inseparable", of the preceding letter is also an important factor. It is seemingly possible always to write medial hamzah independently when the preceding letter is a "separate", unless hamzah is vowelled with kasrah, when yaaʕ-shape is used:

e.g. مَقْرُوءَةٌ [maqruuʕatun], سَاءَلَ [saaʕala],

but مُسَائِلٌ [musaaʕilun].

Similarly, both رُؤُوس and رُءُوس [ruʕuus] are possible forms, while المَرْؤُوس [ʕal marʕuus], where in addition sukuun precedes, is to be preferred to المرئوس:[2] contrast رَئِيس, where kasrah (long) follows.

hamzah as the final consonant of the word, following sukuun and preceding nunation, provides a good illustration of the closely-knit nature of grammatical, phonetic and written systems. Distinction must be made between the nominative and genitive nunations on the one hand, and the accusative nunation on the other. The former are regularly omitted before pause while the latter, at least in a "strict Classical"[3] pronunciation, has a positive phonetic form. This distinction, phonetic and grammatical, is implied in the corresponding written forms.

---

1. ḍammah usually follows. The first variant shown is perhaps to be preferred.

2. But امْرَأَةٌ [ʕimraʕatun], NOT امرءة, and, of course, مَسْأَلَةٌ [masʕalatun], NOT مسئلة. When hamzah is vowelled with fatĥah and follows sukuun or fatĥah (short), no special remark is called for--see above, I,1.

3. For example, in Koranic recitation.

Thus, taking the nominative, hamzah is written independently and the preceding letter has its final shape irrespective of its separate or inseparable nature:

e.g. شَيْءٌ [ʃayʕun], دِفْءٌ [difʕun],
مِلْءٌ [milʕun], نَبِيءٌ [nabiiʕun],[1]
جُزْءٌ [juzʕun], مَرْءٌ [marʕun].

With the accusative nunation, however, the "separate"-"inseparable" differentiation is operative:

e.g. شَيْئًا [ʃayʕan], دِفْئًا [difʕan],
مِلْئًا [milʕan],[2]
but جُزْءً (or جُزْءًا) [juzʕan].

Without final nunation, the distinction is not operative: الشَّيْءُ , الْمِلْءُ .

The account given under ʕalif, yaaʕ and waaw of the method of writing hamzah is by no means exhaustive, but the indications given should provide the student with a model which is generally acceptable.

(ii) <u>Consonantal Function</u>.[3]

As in the case of consonantal yaaʕ, "semi-vocalic" waaw is always initial in a syllable. "Diphthongal" waaw [aw] is always with sukuun, follows fatħah and is either medial or final in a syllable. Doubling of the consonant--indicated by taʃdiid in a "pointed" text--may imply phonetic succession of "diphthongal" and "semi-vocalic" waaw, but a geminated labial consonant is equally possible.

---

1. More commonly نَبِيٌّ [nabiyyun].

2. That neighbouring vowel-units have differential implications as to the writing of hamzah is further illustrated by the practice in some "schools" of distinguishing مِلْئًا [milʕan] and مَلْأً [malʕan].

3. See above, II,5(ii).

Examples:-

6. قَوَّمَ	7. مُقَاوَمٌ	8. اِسْوَدَّ
قوم	مقاوم	اسود
qawwama.	muqaawamun.	ʔiswadda.
9. تَصْوِيرٌ	10. طَوِيلٌ	11. وَرَدَ
تصوير	طويل	ورد
taṣwiirun.	ṭawiilun.	warada.
12. أَوْ	13. يَوْمٌ	14. دَعَوْا
او	يوم	دعوا
ʔaw.	yawmun.	daεaw.
15. مَوْتٌ	16. جَوٌّ	17. جَوْهَرٌ
موت	جو	جوهر
mawtun.	jawwun.	jawharun.

(iii) The waaw of prolongation: اَلْوَاوُ اللَّيِّنَةُ [ʔal waawu llayyinatu]

The third and last of the "aids to reading". The waaw of prolongation is long ḍammah [uu]. It is written in a "pointed" text as ḍammah followed by a waaw which is medial or final in the syllable. Again, as with the yaaʔ of prolongation, a consonant must follow this waaw either in the same syllable or beginning the next. Both "semi-vocalic" and "lengthening" waaw may be preceded by ɖammah--indeed, must be so in the second case--but the former above can--indeed, must--be followed by a vowel. Compare, for example, نُوبٌ [nuubun] and نُوَبٌ [nuwabun].

Again as for yaaʕ,[1] "waaw taʃdiid" preceded by ɖammah is not treated here as long vowel + consonant waaw, although at times there may be justification for this view and a transcribed form [uuw], e.g. زُوِّجَ [zuwwija]

Examples:-

18. تَقُولُ	19. بُيُوتٌ	20. ذُو
تقول	بيوت	ذو
taquulu.	buyuutun.	ðuu.
21. دُونَ	22. شُرُوقٌ	23. شُهُودٌ
دون	شروق	شهود
duuna.	ʃuruuqun.	ʃuhuudun.

1. See above, II,5(iii).

IX.

kaaf, laam.

1. Isolated Forms.

kaaf laam.

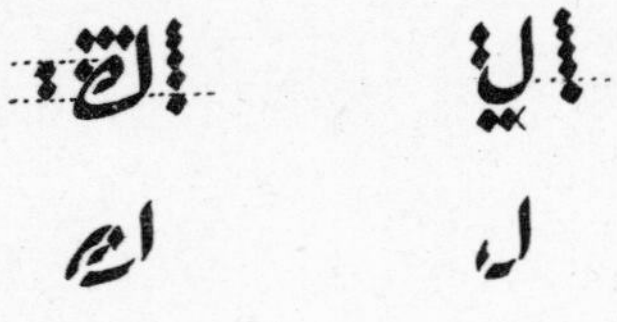

Notes.

(a) The first stroke of both letters is as for ʕalif but longer.

(b) The remaining strokes of laam are as for the last two strokes of siin, ʃiin (i), ṣaad, ḍaad (i).

(c) The second stroke of kaaf resembles the last strokes of baaʕ, taaʕ, θaaʕ, but has greater initial and final curvature.

(d) The third stroke of kaaf, gradually widening, is as for the first stroke of the "box" of ṣaad/ḍaad, but is somewhat thinner and longer.

(e) The last two strokes of kaaf are as for complete daal/ðaal.

(f)  is a regular variant of kaaf, occurring also finally.

2. Initial Forms.

Except before a letter consisting principally of a long vertical stroke, viz. ʕalif, kaaf and laam, the initial and medial forms of kaaf and laam are, if we disregard kaaf's additional stroke, the same.

kaaf is provided with an initial "handle"-stroke, thus: ك. This "handle" should not quite touch the upright. It is marked by slight wave-form, but this should not be exaggerated.

It should be noted that all "upright" strokes in Ruqɛah writing tend to incline slightly forward; just as there would seem to be a natural tendency to slope the writing--in the reverse direction, of course--when we use a Roman script.

A. <u>kaaf</u>

(i) <u>Before ا , ك (m. and f.), ل (m. and f.).</u>

Examples:-

1. كَاتِبٌ

كاتب

kaatibun.

2. كَكَفٍّ

ككف

ka kaffin.

3. كَلَّفَ

كلف

kallafa.

4. كُلٌّ

كل

kullun.

<u>Notes</u>.

(a) (k + ʕalif), (k + k), (k + l) are treated as digraphs. The first element () is for practical purposes as for the "box" of ṣaad/ḍaad. The upright is the next stroke, and the "handle" added finally as shown.

It is important to achieve a sharp corner at the foot of the upright. Rounding is unacceptable.

Thus: 

(b) A variant of (kaaf + ʕalif) is  (). Measurement of the form used in Example 1 above is .

(ii) <u>Before the remaining letters</u>.

Examples:-

5. كَتَبَ

كتب

kataba.

6. كُحْلٌ

كحل

kuħlun.

7. كَذِبٌ

كذب

kaðibun.

8. كَرْبٌ

كرب

karbun.

9. كَسْبٌ

كسب

kasbun.

10. كَصَيِّبٍ

كصيب

ka ṣayyibin.

11. كَظِيمٌ

كظيم

kaðiimun.

12. كَغَيْرِهِ

كغيره

ka ɣayrihi.

13. كَفَلَ

كفل

kafala.

14. كُمٌّ

كم

kummun.

15. كِنٌّ

كن

kinnun.

16. كَهْرَبَةٌ

كهربة

kahrabatun.

17. حاكه 18. كوى 19. حاكى

حاكه كوى حاكى

ħaakahu. kawaa. ħaakaa.

Note. Notice the omission or obscuring of the joining-stroke before medial and final jiim, ħaaʕ, xaaʕ, medial and final miim, and final yaaʕ. This is equally so with laam before these letters (q.v.infra).[1] In cursive form, the joining-line frequently appears before jiim/ħaaʕ/xaaʕ and yaaʕ: thus, كحى , كى .

B. laam.

(i) Before ا.

Example:- 20. لا

لا

laa.

Notes.

(a) The strokes and their order in the shape are as follows:-

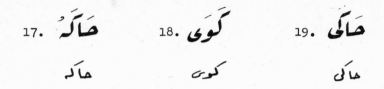

(b) The first stroke is as for the first stroke of daal/ðaal. The second element is a somewhat larger variety of raaʕ/zaay. The final stroke is ʕalif.

Size: 

(c) The Arab grammarians were at pains to establish the number of letters in their alphabet, but they have not always agreed among themselves. Discussion revolved principally

---

1. See above II,2,Note (e), and III,4,Note.

around the relationship between ʕalif and hamzah, and especially on how the ʕalif of prolongation should be regarded.

Certain grammarians were in favour of allotting the ʕalif of prolongation independent status as a twenty-ninth letter of the alphabet, thus clearly separating hamzah and the ʕalif of prolongation. Confusion is perhaps traceable to the late introduction of the letters of prolongation and to a fundamental fact of Arabic phonology, viz. that no syllable may begin with a vowel. All the "other" twenty-eight letters can begin a syllable and are all acrophonic, i.e. the name of each letter begins with that letter. The ʕalif of prolongation was presumably felt to be different; it could not begin a syllable nor could it be called [aaʕ] (sc. without initial glottal stop [ʕaaʕ]): in both cases, hamzah or another consonant must precede. The same difficulty would have been encountered in the cases of the other letters of prolongation, waaw and yaaʕ, but they already had a consonantal function, so their status was assured. The independence of vocalic ʕalif is assured by "supporting" it with laam, whence [laam ʕalif][1] sometimes appears as a twenty-ninth letter.

It is interesting to observe that the alphabet as given to some other languages which use it--Swahili, for example--retains لا as an independent letter.

(ii) <u>Before the remaining letters</u>.

Examples:-

21. لَبِسَ	22. لَحْمٌ	23. لَدْنٌ
لبس	لحم	لدن
labisa.	laħmun.	ladnun.

1. In some Arab countries pronounced as one word [laamaliif].

24. لَزِمَ
lazima.

25. لَسِنَ
lasina.

26. لَصِقَ
laṣiqa.

27. لَطَمَ
laṭama.

28. لَعِبَ
laɛiba.

29. لَفَتَ
lafata.

30. لَكَمَ
lakama.

31. لَمَّا
lammaa.

32. لَنْ
lan.

33. لَهُ
lahu.

34. لَوْحٌ
lawḥun.

35. لِي
lii.

3. Medial Forms.

A. kaaf.

(i) Before ا, ك (m. and f.), ل (m. and f.).

Examples:-

1. شَكَا
ʃakaa.

2. سِكَكٌ
sikakun.

3. نَكَّلَ
nakkala.

(ii) Before the remaining letters.

Examples:-

4. سَكَبَ	5. نَكَحَ	6. نَكِدٌ
سكب	نكح	نكد
sakaba.	nakaħa.	nakidun.
7. أَنْكَرَ	8. نَكَسَ	9. نَكَصَ
أنكر	نكس	نكص
ʕankara.	nakasa.	nakaṣa.
10. نَكَفَ	11. لَكُمْ	12. مَكَّنَ
نكف	لكم	مكن
nakafa.	lakum.	makkana.
13. شَكَّهُ	14. شَكَوْتُ	
شكه	شكوت	
ʃakkahu.	ʃakawtu.	

B. laam.

(i) Before ا.

Example:- 15. بِلَا

بلا

bilaa.

Notes.

(a) A common variant when laam + ʕalif follow an inseparable letter is بلا (بلا) with curvature at the top of the up-right before the final sweep is made for laam.

(b) Form (ii) of initial baaʕ, taaʕ, θaaʕ, nuun, yaaʕ, is, of course, a variant before لـ. Thus:- بلا

(ii) Before the remaining letters.

Examples:-

16. قَلَبَ قلب qalaba.	17. فَلَحَ فلح falaħa.	18. قَلَّدَ قلد qallada.
19. حَلَزُون حلزون ħalazuun.	20. غَلَسٌ غلس ɣalasun.	21. خِلْصٌ خلص xilṣun.
22. غَلِطَ غلط ɣaliṭa.	23. عَلَفَ علف ɛalafa.	24. عَلَّقَ علق ɛallaqa.
25. عَلَّكَ علك ɛallaka.	26. عَلَّلَ علل ɛallala.	27. عَلَّمَ علم ɛallama.

28. عَلَنٌ	29. عَلَّهُ	30. عَلَّهُمْ
علن	عله	علهم
ɛalanun.	ɛallahu.	ɛallahum.
31. عَلَوْتُ	32. عَلِيٌّ	
علوت	علي	
ɛalawtu.	ɛaliyyun.	

4. Final Forms.

A. <u>kaaf</u>.

Examples:-

1. بِكَ	2. حَكَّ	3. أَمْسَكَ
بك	حك	أمسك
bika.	ħakka.	ʔamsaka.
4. نَصُّكَ	5. غَلَطُكَ	6. دَعْكَ
نصك	غلطك	دعك
naṣṣuka.	ɣalaṭuka.	daɛka.
7. سَفَكَ	8. عَلَّكَ	9. عَمُّكَ
سفك	علك	عمك
safaka.	ɛallaka.	ɛammuka.

10. أَنْهَكَ

أنهك

ʕanhaka.

B. laam.

Examples:-

11. قَبِلَ

قبل

qabila.

12. كُحْلٌ

كحل

kuħlun.

13. تَوَسَّلَ

توسل

tawassala.

14. تَوَصَّلَ

توصل

tawaṣṣala.

15. رَطْلٌ

رطل

raṭlun.

16. بَغْلٌ

بغل

baɣlun.

17. نَقَلَ

نقل

naqala.

18. كَلْكَلٌ

كلكل

kalkalun.

19. عَمِلَ

عمل

ɛamila.

20. كَهْلٌ

كهل

kahlun.

X.

miim.

1. Isolated Form.

Apart from being rather smaller and less horizontally disposed, the first three strokes of isolated miim are as for medial ɛayn/ɣayn.

 1.

(i) (ii) (iii)

The continuation of the third stroke is as follows:-

rounded.  rounded.

For the final stroke the nib is rotated to a vertical position in order to achieve a thin stroke:-

2. Initial Form: ()

Examples:-

1. 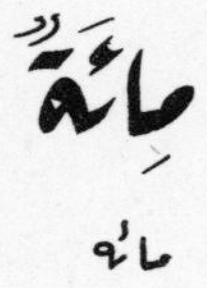 2.

2. 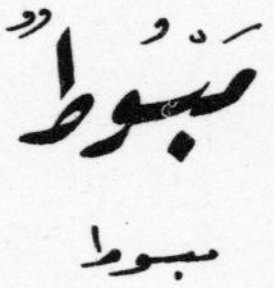

3. 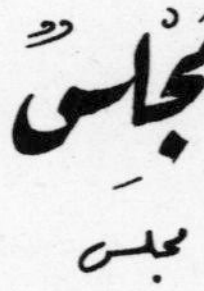

miʕatun. mabsuuṭun. majlisun.

---

1. See above, VII,3.

2. ʕalif here is archaic and not pronounced. The word is often written مئة .

4. مَدِينَةٌ	5. مَرَّ	6. مَسَحَ
مدينة	مر	مسح
madiinatun.	marra.	masaħa.
7. مِصْرُ	8. مَطَرٌ	9. مَعَ
مصر	مطر	مع
miṣru.	maṭarun.	maɛa.
10. مَفْتُوحٌ	11. أَمْكَنَ	12. مَلَأَ
مفتوح	أمكن	ملأ
maftuuħun.	ʕamkana.	malaʕa.
13. مِمَّا	14. مِنْ	15. مِهْنَةٌ
مما	من	مهنة
mimmaa.	min.	mihnatun.
16. أُمَّةٌ	17. مَوْجٌ	18. هَرَمِي
أمة	موج	هرمي
ʕummatun.	mawjun.	haramii.

<u>Note</u>: In cursive writing the "blob" of miim frequently resembles faaʕ. The letter appears often in the form of a small circle or triangle, e.g. موج .

3. Medial Form: (ـمـ - ـمـ)

Examples:-

1. مِمَّا	2. قُمْتُ	3. سَمِجٌ
مما	قمت	سمج
mimmaa.	qumtu.	samijun.
4. سَمَّدَ	5. أَسْمَرُ	6. لَمَسَ
سمد	أسمر	لمس
sammada.	ʔasmaru.	lamasa.
7. قَمَصَ	8. سَمَطَ	9. عُمْقٌ
قمص	سمط	عمق
qamaṣa.	samaṭa.	ʕumqun.
10. سَمَكٌ	11. سَمَلَ	12. سَمَّمَ
سمك	سمل	سمم
samakun.	samala.	sammama.
13. سِمَنٌ	14. اِسْمُهُ	15. اِسْمُهُمْ
سمن	اسمه	اسمهم
simanun.	ʔismuhu.	ʔismuhum.

16. يُسَمُّونَ   17. اِسْمِي

يسمون   اسمي

yusammuuna.   ʕismii.

<u>Notes</u>.

(a) At the conclusion of the preceding joining-line, a short stroke is drawn downwards in the direction of minimum thickness, before commencing the "head" of miim: , . The same thing is done in order to accommodate the "bend-back" before medial and final jiim/ħaaʕ/xaaʕ and final yaaʕ. This does not apply when the preceding letter is kaaf or laam.[1]

(b) In cursive form, it is often difficult to distinguish between medial miim and medial jiim/ħaaʕ/xaaʕ.

4. <u>Final Form.</u>

Examples:-

1. قَائِمٌ   2. رَحِمَ   3. قَسَمَ

قائم   رحم   قسم

qaaʕimun.   raħima.   qasama.

4. فَصَمَ   5. لَطَمَ   6. لَغَمٌ

فصم   لطم   لغم

faʂama.   laʈama.   laɣamun.

---

1. See above, IX,2,A(ii), Note.

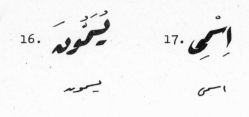

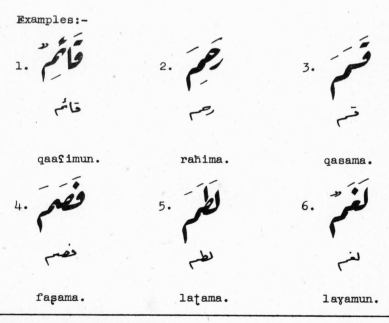

7. فَمٌ

فم

famun.

8. كُمٌّ

كم

kummun.

9. لَمْ

لم

lam.

10. هُمْ

هم

hum.

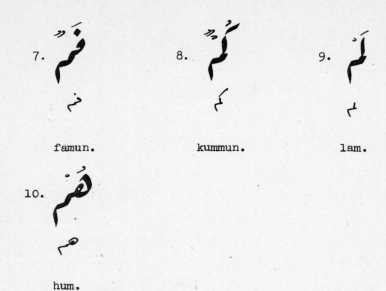

XI.

haaʕ.

Of all the Arabic letters, haaʕ is probably the least uniform as to shape. Medial and final haaʕ each have two variant forms. There is thus a total of six shapes:-

Isolated. Initial. Medial. Final.

1. Isolated Form.

This form of the letter is acorn-shaped. The curvature of the upper half is much more marked than that of the lower. The shape is perhaps best made in two halves:  and - .

2. Initial Form.

The first stroke of the shape is approximately as for the three-dots symbol (). The second stroke resembles ʕalif but is more sloping and, contrary to ʕalif, is slightly curved. The remainder of the shape may be looked upon as medial faaʕ/qaaf. In this "isolated" form, the shape is given a final "tail".

Examples:-

1. 

هائم

haaʕimun.

2. 

هبه

habhu.

3. 

هجم

hajama.

4. هَدَرَ

هدر

hadara.

5. أَهْرَقَ

أهرق

ʕahraqa.

6. هَشَّ

هش

haʃʃa.

7. هَصَرَ

هصر

haṣara.

8. هَطَلَ

هطل

haṭala.

9. هَفَا

هفا

hafaa.

10. هَٰكَذَا

هٰكذا

haakaðaa.

11. هَلْ

هل

hal.

12. هَمَّ

هم

hamma.

13. هُنَّ

هن

hunna.

14. جَاهُهُ

جاهه

jaahuhu.

15. هُوَ

هو

huwa.

16. هِيَ

هي

hiya.

3. Medial Form.

There are two variant shapes of medial haaʕ. They are (i)  and (ii) .

The two are quite interchangeable in Arabic,[1] but form (ii) is the commoner and therefore to be preferred. It is almost exclusively used in the cursive writing of Ruqɛah. Before this second form, the joining-line from the preceding letter is regularly dispensed with in cursive form, and may equally be omitted in the calligraphic rendering. In the calligraphic examples given below, however, a preceding joining-line has been included wherever possible.

Thus, for Example 5 below, there are three possible renderings:- (i)  (ii)  (iii) 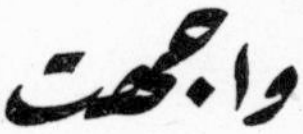

The method of joining medial haaʕ form (ii) to a following letter varies with the letter.

(i) Before ع (m. and f.), م (m. and f.), ى (f.).

Examples:-

1. 

2. 

3. 

nahaja. ṭahhama. fa hiya.

Note: The "bridge" junction would appear optional before miim, but is compulsory before jiim/ħaaʕ/xaaʕ and final yaaʕ.

---

1. It is interesting to observe that Urdu has profited from the existence of these two variants, and has allotted a clearly defined function to each. Thus, "two-eyed h"--as ھ is called in the Indian continent--is used to point a very significant phonological feature of the language, symbolising the aspiration of a preceding plosive consonant; the second variant symbolises breathiness, initial, final or throughout the syllable.

(ii) <u>Before the remaining letters</u>.

Examples:-

4. بِهَا

بها

bihaa.

5. وَاجَهْتُ

واجهت

waajahtu.

6. سُهْدٌ

سهد

suhdun.

7. صَهَرَ

صهر

ṣahara.

8. مُهْرٌ

مهر

muhrun.

9. نَهَسَ

نهس

nahaʃa.

10. نَهَضَ

نهض

nahaḍa.

11. لَهَفَ

لهف

lahafa.

12. رَفَّهَكَ

رفهك

raffahaka.

13. كَهْلٌ

كهل

kahlun.

14. عِهْنٌ

عهن

ɛihnun.

15. رَفَّهَهُ

رفهه

raffahahu.

16. فَهُوَ

فهو

fa huwa.

Note. The junction of the preceding joining-line and the first stroke of medial haaʕ is inevitably slightly rounded, in the calligraphic form, since the first stroke of haaʕ has slight curvature; in cursive form, however, the sweep-down from the preceding letter is usually without interruption.

4. Final Form.

There are two variant final forms of haaʕ:-

(i) (ii)

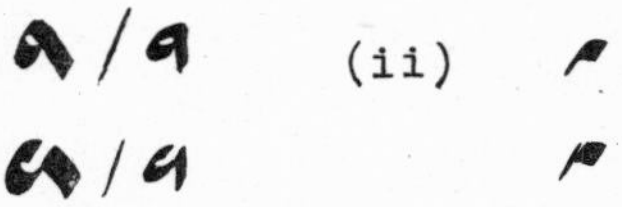

Form (ii) has a slight ascent before the final downstroke and the joining-line is characterised by general curvature. The thin downstroke is on the face of it all that belongs to final haaʕ in this form, but the shape of the preceding joining-line is characteristic.

taaʕ marbuuṭah.

The final and isolated forms of haaʕ, with the addition of the two dots of taaʕ, are used for the feminine and unit-ending -atun. This form ة is called "taaʕun marbuuṭatun" (تاءٌ مربوطةٌ) as distinct from "taaʕun maftuuħatun" (تاءٌ مفتوحةٌ) or "taaʕun ṭawiilatun" (تاءٌ طويلةٌ)-- sc. ت . The first term refers apparently to the phonetic function of the shape ة , while the other two refer simply to the shape ت .

The feminine ending in the nominative and genitive forms usually has the phonetic form -ah when final, i.e. before pause. When the termination is no longer final, [t + vowel (+ nunation)] returns, hence "linking (lit. "linked") t".

Examples:-

1. رَبُّهُ (ربه)   2. حُجَّةٌ (حجة)   3. بَأْسُهُ (بأسه)

(ربه) ربـ   (حجة) حجـة   (بأسه) بأسـ

rabbuhu.   ħujjatun.   baʕsuhu.

4. قِصَّةٌ (قصة)   5. غَلْطَةٌ (غلطه)   6. دَعَةٌ (دعة)

(قصة) قصـة   (غلطة) غلطـة   (دعة) دعـة

qiṣṣatun.   ɣalṭatun.   daɛatun.

7. دَفَّةٌ (دفة)   8. دَكَّةٌ (دكة)   9. عَادِلَةٌ (عادلة)

(دفة) دفـة   (دكة) دكـة   (عادلة) عادلـة

daffatun.   dakkatun.   ɛaadilatun.

10. عَمَّةٌ (عمة)   11. وَاجَهَهُ (واجهه)

(عمة) عمـة   (واجهه) واجـه

ɛammaŧun.   waajahahu.

XII.

CONCLUSION.

1. Multiliteral Words.

The systematisation of the Arabic letters' shapes has been exemplified for the most part in word-shapes of three letters; the principles set forth are, of course, equally applicable to all words, whatever their number of component letters.

Examples:-

1. يَسْتَخْدِمُونَ

يستخدمون

yastaxdimuuna.

2. يَتَبَنَّوْنَ

يتبنون

yatabannawna.

3. يَتَنَجَّعُونَ [1]

يتنجعون

yatanajjaɛuuna.

4. يَتَصَنَّعُونَ

يتصنعون

yataṣannaɛuuna.

5. يَسْتَعْظِمُونَ

يستعظمون

yastaɛðimuuna.

6. مُسْتَقْبِلُونَ

مستقبلون

mustaqbiluuna.

7. سَيَسْتَعْظِمُونَ

سيستعظمون

sayastaɛðimuuna.

8. اَلْقُسْطَنْطِينِيَّةُ

القسطنطينية

ʕal qusṭanṭiiniyyatu.

---

1. The "special" shape--see above, II,3(iii)--is not used for the second letter when the third letter has the special "bridge" shape before jiim, miim and final yaaʕ.

2. The Letters In Relation To The Line Of Writing.

We are trained as children to write our native roman scripts in strict relation to a horizontal line across the page. We are not allowed to perpetrate, say:-

"He came straight to the point."

This horizontal line--imaginary, of course--is equally necessary to the acceptable writing of Arabic, yet our efforts all to often approximate to the above multi-directional monstrosity.

The lowest edge of most of the Arabic letters in isolation should touch the "line"; some, however, - viz. jiim/ħaaʕ/xaaʕ, ɛayn/ɣayn, miim and medial haaʕ (form ii) - partially descend below the line. The lower curved strokes of siin/ʃiin (forms i and ii), and ʂaad/ɖaad (forms i and ii) may also be projected below the line.

The relation of shapes to the line is as follows:-

This is not, however, the complete story. Given that, in Ruqɛah, the angle of the joining-line remains for practical purposes constant (), it becomes important to consider whether a following letter involves descent in comparison with the preceding letter or letters. The structure as a whole of the Arabic written word has already been stressed; it is no less important for our present purpose. Thus the miim of موت [mawt] must be written at a higher level than the miim of مات [maata] because of the descent required in the case of following و, compared with the ascent of following ا. The effect of following descent may not be confined to the preceding letter, but can be felt at a considerable distance. Thus the waaw of مستقبلون [mustaqbiluuna] influences the general and individual evel of six letters preceding it. It is necessary, therefore, to lan ahead. Take, for example, the name [ʕibraahiimu]; before writ-ng it, the student should consider the facts that:

(i) ʕalif must touch "the line".

(ii) raaʕ must touch "the line"; therefore, baaʕ must be started fairly high.

(iii) miim is a "descender"; therefore, haaʕ must be "high".

Thus:- ابراهيم [1]

There are occasions when the calligrapher, exercising the rerogative of his art, transposes letters,[2] words or bits of words, lacing them, for example, above or below other letters or words in rder, say, to fill up an offending blank space. Such occasions are, owever, comparatively rare in Ruqɛah, and the practice is to be voided, at least by the beginner.

In cursive writing, the need for greater speed produces nomalies, but an overall adherence to the principles outlined above s still maintained.

A quick appreciation of the accuracy with which these prin-iples have been followed can be obtained by rotating the paper or ook through 90° and, with the eye on the level of the paper, looking long the lines.

3. The Numerals.

The numerals, in their calligraphic and cursive forms, are as follows:-

٠ ١ ٢ ٣ ٤ ٥ ٦ ٧ ٨ ٩

٠ ١ ٢ ٣ ٤ ٥ ٦ ٧ ٨ ٩

(ṣifrun, waaħidun, ʕiΘnaani, ΘalaaΘatun, ʕarbaɛatun, xamsatun, sitt-atun, sabɛatun, Θamaaniyatun, tisɛatun, ɛaʃaratun).

---

1. For the position of the second ʕalif, see I,3(iv).

2. Thus ʕalif--in rather shortened form--is subject to frequent levitation.

4. We have noted certain possibilities of confusion in the cursive form of Ruqɛah, but in the main, the principle of differentiation is applicable equally to the written as to the spoken form of a language, however much individual variation is found from writer to writer. Thus, the highest common factor of all varieties of medial baaʕ/taaʕ/θaaʕ/nuun/yaaʕ, is prominence above the surrounding joining-lines; medial jiim/ħaaʕ/xaaʕ, and medial miim are characterised by descent from the level of the preceding joining-line and by a "bending-back"[1] before proceeding to the next letter; the unbroken nature of the stroke and its relative length reveal initial and medial siin/ʃiin,[2] and so on.

5. In both the calligraphic and cursive forms, but especially in the former, care must be taken to ensure, not only that the individual parts of a letter are so proportioned as to constitute an acceptable whole, but also that the letters are in correct mutual proportion within the word, and the word in turn within the word-group.

6. Remember that, when using a reed-pen, the size of your letters depends upon the width to which the nib has been cut. The narrower the nib, the smaller the letter and word. Remember, too, the relatively constant angle at which the nib is maintained; this fact, together with the more or less constant slope of the joining-strokes,

---

1. This "bend-back" may sometimes appear in cursive writing as an approximately vertical stroke, but it is never drawn from right to left: or but never).

2. A long unbroken line is sometimes used for purely artistic effect between two letters - most frequently perhaps before final haaʕ (ه) This practice, however, is relatively rare, and the stroke is usually distinguishable from siin/ʃiin by the greater length of stroke employed.

is responsible for producing effects of parallelism, deviation from which is unacceptable.

7. Finally, here are a few random examples--frequently seen--of how NOT to write Arabic. Their demerits are clearly due to an unenlightened and unsuccessful imitation of Nasx forms.

(المبتدأ)	المبتدأ	(نهار)	نهار	(حارة)	حارة
(فتح)	فتح	(شهور)	شهور	(مظلم)	مظلم
(سائح)	سائح	(كلاب)	كلاب	(اثنتان)	اثنتان
(بالكل)	بالكل	(صحراء)	صحراء	(إمرؤ)	إمرؤ
(صحيح)	صحيح	(ريح)	ريح	(لما)	لما
(صاحب)	صاحب	(شمس)	شمس	(اسم)	اسم
(شيخ)	شيخ	(حجر)	حجر	(لعجمهم)	لعجمهم
(الهجاء)	الهجاء	(عين)	عين	(للحق)	للحق
(كسر)	كسر	(مفتاح)	مفتاح	(شجر)	شجر
(لكن)	لكن	(زيد)	زيد	(أبن)	أبن
(زكاة)	زكاة	(ضرب)	ضرب	(مع السلامة)	مع السلامة
(بحور)	بحور	(حم)	حم	(مجتهد)	مجتهد
(ميت)	ميت	(أبيض)	أبيض	(كبير)	كبير
(طالع)	طالع	(ترجم)	ترجم	(القاضي)	القاضي
(مملوك)	مملوك	(جزيرة)	جزيرة	(حسن)	حسن
(ميزان)	ميزان	(سوق)	سوق	(عريض)	عريض

APPENDIX A.[1]

1.(a) 69

سأل أحمد ملاحا: "أين مات أبوك؟" فأجاب
الملاح: "في مركب كان يركبه في البحر" "وأين
مات جدك؟" "هو أيضا مات في مركب كان
يركبه في البحر" "ولا تخاف أن تركب مركبا بعد
ذلك؟" فقال الملاح: "أين مات أبوك؟"
"على فراش" "وجدك؟" "على فراش" "وأنت
لا تخاف أن تنام على الفراش بعد ذلك؟"

(b)

سأل أحمد ملاحا: "أين مات أبوك؟" فأجاب الملاح: "في مركب
كان يركبه في البحر" "وأين مات جدك؟" "هو أيضا مات في مركب
كان يركبه في البحر" "ولا تخاف أن تركب مركبا بعد ذلك؟" فقال
الملاح: "أين مات أبوك؟" "على فراش" "وجدك؟" "على فراش" "وأنت
لا تخاف أن تنام على الفراش بعد ذلك؟"

1. The following specimen passages have been selected from ARABIC LANGUAGE AND GRAMMAR by J. Kapliwatzky.

(c)

saʕala ʕaħmadu mallaaħan: ‘ʕayna maata ʕabuukaʔ’ fa ʕajaaba l mallaaħu: ‘fii markabin kaana yarkabuhu fii l baħri.’ ‘wa ʕayna maata jaddukaʔ’ ‘huwa ʕayɖan maata fii markabin kaana yarkabuhu fii l baħri.’ ‘wa laa taxaafu ʕan tarkaba markaban baεda ðaalikaʔ’ fa qaala l mallaaħu: ‘ʕayna maata ʕabuukaʔ’ ‘εalaa firaaʃihi.’ ‘wa jaddukaʔ’ ‘εalaa firaaʃihi.’ ‘wa ʕanta laa taxaafu ʕan tanaama εalaa l firaaʃi baεda ðaalikaʔ’

-oOo-

2.(a)

هرتان وجدتا قطعة جبن وذهبتا بها إلى
القرد كي يقسمها بينهما فأخذ القرد الجبنة
وقسمها إلى قسمين أحدهما أكبر من الآخر ثم
وضع كل واحد من القسمين في كفة من ميزانه
فرجح القسم الأكبر فأخذ منه قليلا بأسنانه
وأكله وقال: "أريد أن أساويه بالأصغر"
ولكن إذ كان ما أخذه منه أكثر من اللازم
رجح الأصغر ففعل بهذا ما فعله بذلك ثم

فعل بذلك ما فعله بهذا وما زال يأكل مما
رجح من القسمين حتى أكل الجبنة كلها

(b)

هرتان وجدتا قطعة جبن وذهبتا بها إلى القرد كي يقسمها بينهما
فأخذ القرد الجبنة وقسمها إلى قسمين أحدهما أكبر من الآخر ثم وضع
كل واحد من القسمين في كفة من ميزانه فرجح القسم الأكبر فأخذ منه
قليلا بأسنانه وأكله وقال: "أريد أن أساويه بالأصغر" ولكن
إذ كان ما أخذه منه أكثر من اللازم رجح الأصغر ففعل بهذا ما
فعله بذلك ثم فعل بذلك ما فعله بهذا وما زال يأكل مما رجح من
القسمين حتى أكل الجبنة كلها

(c)

hirrataani wajadataa qiṭɛata jubnin wa ðahabataa bihaa ʔilaa l qirdi kay yaqsimahaa baynahumaa. fa ʔaxaða l qirdu l jubnata wa qasamahaa ʔilaa qismayni ʔaħaduhumaa ʔakbaru min a l ʔaaxari. θumma waḍaɛa kulla waaħidin min a l qismayni fii kaffatin min miizaanihi fa rajaħa l qismu l ʔakbaru fa ʔaxaða minhu qaliilan bi ʔasnaanihi wa ʔakalahu wa qaala: 'ʔuriidu ʔan ʔusaawiyahu bi l ʔaṣɣari.' walaakin ʔið kaana maa ʔaxaðahu minhu ʔakθara min a l laazimi rajaħa l ʔaṣɣaru fa faɛala bi haaðaa maa faɛalahu bi ðaalika θumma faɛala bi ðaalika maa faɛalahu bi haaðaa wa maa zaala yaʔkulu mimmaa rajaħa min a l qismayni ħattaa ʔakala l jubnata kullahaa.

-oOo-

3.(a) 128

فتح رجل دكان سمك وعلق فوق بابه لوحا

صغيرا كتب عليه "هنا يباع السمك" فجاء أحد

أصدقائه وقال له: "لماذا كتبت على اللوح

كلمة 'هنا' ألا يباع السمك إلا في دكانك؟"

فحذف صاحب الدكان كلمة 'هنا' ثم جاء

صديق آخر فقال لصاحب الدكان: "لماذا

كتبت على اللوح كلمة 'يباع' ألا يفهم الناس

أنك لا توزع السمك مجانا؟" فحذف كلمة 'يباع'

ثم جاء صديق ثالث وقال: "لماذا كتبت

كلمة 'السمك' ألا يراه الناس ولا يشمونه؟"

فنزع صاحب الدكان اللوح

(b)

فتح رجل دكان سمك وعلق فوق بابه لوحا صغيرا كتب عليه

"هنا يباع السمك" فجاء أحد أصدقائه وقال له: "لماذا كتبت على

اللوح كلمة 'هنا' ألا يباع السمك إلا في دكانك؟" فحذف صاحب

الدكان كلمة 'هنا' ثم جاء صديق آخر فقال لصاحب الدكان:

"لماذا كتبت على اللوح كلمة 'يباع' ألا يفهم الناس أنك لا توزع

السمك مجانا؟" فحذف كلمة 'يباع' ثم جاء صديق ثالث وقال:

"لماذا كتبت كلمة 'السمك' ألا يراه الناس ولا يشمونه؟"

فنزع صاحب الدكان اللوح

(c)

fataħa rajulun dukkaana samakin wa ɛallaqa fawqa baabihi lawħan ṣaɣiiran kutiba ɛalayhi: ʻhunaa yubaaɛu l samaku.ʼ fa jaaʔa ʔaħadu ʔaṣdiqaaʔihi wa qaala lahu: ʻlimaaðaa katabta ɛalaa l lawħi kalimata 'hunaa'. ʔa laa yubaaɛu l samaku ʔillaa fii dukkaanikaʔʼ fa ħaðafa ṣaaħibu l dukkaani kalimata 'hunaa'. θumma jaaʔa ṣadiiqun ʔaaxaru fa qaala li ṣaaħibi l dukkaani: ʻlimaaðaa katabta ɛalaa l lawħi kalimata 'yubaaɛu'. ʔa laa yafhamu l naasu ʔannaka laa τuwazziɛu l samaka majjaananʔʼ fa ħaðafa kalimata 'yubaaɛu'. θumma jaaʔa ṣadiiqun θaaliθun wa qaala: ʻlimaaðaa katabta kalimata '[ʔa]l samaku' ʔa laa yaraahu l naasu wa laa yaʃummuunahuʔʼ fa nazaɛa ṣaaħibu l dukkaani l lawħa.

-oOo-

4.(a) 137

رأى ملك شيخا واحدا يغرس نخلا فقال له:

" أيها الشيخ، أتؤمل أن تأكل من ثمر هذا النخل

وهو لا يثمر إلا بعد سنين كثيرة؟" فقال الشيخ:

"أغرس النخل ليأكل أحفادي من ثمره كما أكلت

أنا مما غرس جدي" فاستحسن الملك ذلك وأعطاه

عشرين دينارا فأخذها الشيخ وقال: "أيها الملك

لقد أكلت أنا بنفسي من ثمر هذا النخل"

فتعجب الملك من كلامه وأعطاه عشرين دينارا

أخرى فأخذها الشيخ وقال: "أيها الملك وأعجب

من كل شيء أن النخل قد أثمر السنة مرتين"

فتعجب الملك من كلامه وأعطاه عشرين

دينارا أخرى

(b)

رأى ملك شيخا واحدا يغرس نخلا فقال له: "أيها الشيخ أتؤمل أن

تأكل من ثمر هذا النخل وهو لا يثمر إلا بعد سنين كثيرة؟" فقال

الشيخ: "أغرس النخل ليأكل أحفادي من ثمره كما أكلت أنا مما غرس

جدي" فاستحسن الملك ذلك وأعطاه عشرين دينارا فأخذها الشيخ

وقال: "أيها الملك لقد أكلت أنا بنفسي من ثمر هذا النخل"

فتعجب الملك من كلامه وأعطاه عشرين دينارا أخرى فأخذها

الشيخ وقال: "أيها الملك وأعجب من كل شيء أن النخل قد أثمر

السنة مرتين" فتعجب الملك من كلامه وأعطاه عشرين دينارا أخرى

(c)

raʔaa malikun ʃayxan waaħidan yaɣrisu naxlan fa qaala lahu. ‘ʔayyuhaa l ʃayxu. ʔa tuʔammilu ʔan taʔkula min θamari haaðaa l naxli wa huwa laa yuθmiru ʔillaa baɛda siniina kaθiiratin?’ fa qaala l ʃayxu: ‘ʔaɣrisu l naxla li yaʔkula ʔaħfaadii min θamarihi kamaa ʔakaltu ʔana mimmaa ɣarasa jaddii.’ fa staħsana l maliku ðaalika wa ʔaɛʈaahu ɛiʃriina diinaaran fa ʔaxaðahaa l ʃayxu wa qaala. ‘ʔayyuhaa l maliku. laqad ʔakaltu ʔana binafsii min θamari haaðaa l naxli.’ fa taɛajjaba l maliku min kalaamihi wa ʔaɛʈaahu ɛiʃriina diinaaran ʔuxraa fa ʔaxaðahaa l ʃayxu wa qaala: ‘ʔayyuhaa l maliku. wa ʔaɛjabu min kulli ʃayʔin ʔanna l naxla qad ʔaθmara l sanata marratayni.’ fa taɛajjaba l maliku min kalaamihi wa ʔaɛʈaahu ɛiʃriina diinaaran ʔuxraa.

-oOo-

5.(a) 144

حمل رجل مرة حزمة حطب من الغابة القريبة
إلى بيته فثقلت عليه فلما تعب من حملها
رمى بها عن كتفه ودعا على نفسه بالموت
فشخص له الموت وقال: "ها أنا ذا لماذا
دعوتني؟" فقال الرجل: "دعوتك لتحملني
حزمة الحطب هذه على كتفي"

(b)

حمل رجل مرة حزمة حطب من الغابة القريبة إلى بيته فثقلت
عليه فلما تعب من حملها رمى بها عن كتفه ودعا على نفسه بالموت
فشخص له الموت وقال: "ها أنا ذا لماذا دعوتني؟" فقال الرجل:
"دعوتك لتحملني حزمة الحطب هذه على كتفي"

(c)

ħamala rajulun marratan ħuzmata ħaţabin min a l ɣaabati l qariibati ʔilaa baytihi fa θaqulat ʕalayhi. fa lammaa taʕiba min ħamlihaa ramaa bihaa ʕan katifihi wa daʕaa ʕalaa nafsihi bi l mawti. fa ʃaxaşa lahu l mawtu wa qaala: ‘haa ʔana ðaa. limaaða daʕawtanii?’

fa qaala l rajulu: ‘daɛawtuka li tuħammilanii ħuzmata l ħaṭabi haaðihi ɛalaa katifii.’

-oOo-

6.(a) 122

كان صياد يصيد عصافير في يوم بارد فكان
يذبحها والدموع تسيل من عينيه من شدة البرد
فقال أحد العصافير لصاحبه: "لا تخف من
هذا الرجل ألا تراه يبكي؟" فقال له الآخر
"لا تنظر إلى دموعه بل إلى ما تصنع يداه"

(b)

كان صياد يصيد عصافير في يوم بارد فكان يذبحها والدموع
تسيل من عينيه من شدة البرد فقال أحد العصافير لصاحبه:
"لا تخف من هذا الرجل ألا تراه يبكي؟" فقال له الآخر: "لا تنظر
إلى دموعه بل إلى ما تصنع يداه"

(c)

kaana ṣayyaadun yaṣiidu ɛaṣaafiira fii yawmin baaridin fa kaana yaðbaħuhaa wa l dumuuɛu tasiilu min ɛaynayhi min ʃiddati l bardi. fa qaala ʔaħadu l ɛaṣaafiiri li ṣaaħibihi: ‘laa taxaf min haaðaa l rajuli. ʔa laa taraahu yabkii?’ fa qaala lahu l ʔaaxaru: ‘laa tanður ʔilaa dumuuɛihi bal ʔilaa maa taṣnaɛu yadaahu.’

7.(a) 113

كان لرجل ببغاء جميلة تعرف الكلام وإذا

مر بها رجل قالت له "نهارك سعيد يا أخى"

وكانت تخرج إلى البستان بعد الظهر وتنتظر

صاحبها إلى أن يرجع من دكانه وعندما تراه

كانت تقول "يا عمى خذنى إلى البيت"

فضاعت الببغاء يوما فكان صاحبها يسأل

كل الناس عنها فقال له أحد الرجال: "إنى

سمعت صوت ببغاء فى بيت جارى"

فذهب صاحب الببغاء إلى جار ذلك

الرجل وسأله عن الببغاء فلما سمعت

صوت صاحبها قالت: "يا عمى خذنى إلى

البيت" فدخل الرجل وأخذها من بيت السارق

(b)

كان لرجل ببغاء جميلة تعرف الكلام وإذا مر بها رجل قالت

له "نهارك سعيد يا أخي" وكانت تخرج إلى البستان بعد الظهر

وتنتظر صاحبها إلى أن يرجع من دكانه وعندما تراه كانت تقول

"يا عمي خذني إلى البيت" فضاعت الببغاء يوما فكان صاحبها

يسأل كل الناس عنها فقال له أحد الرجال: "إني سمعت صوت

ببغاء في بيت جاري" فذهب صاحب الببغاء إلى جار ذلك

الرجل وسأله عن الببغاء فلما سمعت صوت صاحبها قالت:

"يا عمي خذني إلى البيت" فدخل الرجل وأخذها من بيت السارق

(c)

kaana li rajulin babaɣaaʔu jamiilatun taʕrifu l kalaama wa ʔiðaa mərra bihaa rajulun qaalat lahu: ‘nahaaruka saʕiidun yaa ʔaxii.’ wa kaanat taxruju ʔilaa l bustaani baʕda l ðuhri wa tantaðiru ṣaaħibahaa ʔilaa ʔan yarjiʕa min dukkaanihi wa ʕindamaa taraahu kaanat taquulu: ‘yaa ʕammii xuðnii ʔilaa l bayti.’ fa ḍaaʕat i l babaɣaaʔu yawman fa kaana ṣaaħibuhaa yasʔalu kulla l naasi ʕanhaa fa qaala lahu ʔaħadu l rijaali: ‘ʔinnii samiʕtu ṣawta babaɣaaʔa fii bayti jaarii.’ fa ðahaba ṣaaħibu l babaɣaaʔi ʔilaa jaari ðaalika l rajuli wa saʔalahu ʕan i l babaɣaaʔi. fa lammaa samiʕat ṣawta ṣaaħibihaa qaalat: ‘yaa ʕammii xuðnii ʔilaa l bayti.’ fa daxala l rajulu wa ʔaxaðahaa min bayti l saariqi.

-oOo-

3.(a) [Abridged from the original] 142

أنشئت جمعية فى إحدى المدن غايتها محاربة

الأمية ففتحت هذه الجمعية مدارس ليلية

فى القرى والمدن لتعليم الفلاحين والعمال

القراءة والكتابة فأرسلت هذه الجمعية يوما

مفتشا إلى إحدى القرى يحمل هدايا للذين

يتعلمون فى هذه المدارس الليلية تشجيعا

لهم فاجتمع الفلاحون حوله فدعا المفتش

امرأة منهم وطلب منها أن تقرأ كلمة

أشار إليها فى كتاب كان فى يده فقرأت

بصوت عال "منديل" فقال لها "أحسنت"

وأعطاها منديلا ثم دعا رجلا وطلب منه

أن يقرأ كلمة أشار إليها فقرأ بسرعة

"ثور" وكانت الكلمة شيئا آخر فقال له

المفتش "أنظر جيدا واقرأ" فنظر الرجل

مرة أخرى وقال "ثور" فقامت زوجته

وقالت "زوجي يحسن القراءة ولكنه في

حاجة شديدة إلى ثور يحرث به الأرض"

(b)

أنشئت جمعية في إحدى المدن غايتها محاربة الأمية ففتحت

هذه الجمعية مدارس ليلية في القرى والمدن لتعليم الفلاحين

والعمال القراءة والكتابة فأرسلت هذه الجمعية يوما مفتشا

إلى إحدى القرى يحمل هدايا للذين يتعلمون في هذه المدارس

الليلية تشجيعا لهم فاجتمع الفلاحون حوله فدعا المفتش

امرأة منهم وطلب منها أن تقرأ كلمة أشار إليها في

كتاب كان في يده فقرأت بصوت عال "منديل" فقال لها

"أحسنت" وأعطاها منديلا ثم دعا رجلا وطلب منه أن

يقرأ كلمة أشار إليها فقرأ بسرعة "ثور" وكانت الكلمة

شيئا آخر فقال له المفتش "أنظر جيدا واقرأ" فنظر الرجل

مرة اخرى وقال "ثور" فقامت زوجته وقالت "زوجي يحسن القراءة

ولكنه في حاجة شديدة الى ثور يحرث به الارض"

(c)

ʔunʃiʔat jamɛiyyatun fii ʔiħdaa l muduni ɣaayatu-haa muħaarabatu l ʔummiyyati fa fataħat haaðihi l jam-ɛiyyatu madaarisa layliyyatan fii l quraa wa l muduni li taɛliimi l fallaaħiina wa l ɛummaali l qiraaʔata wa l kitaabata fa ʔarsalat haaðihi l jamɛiyyatu yawman mufattiʃan ʔilaa ʔiħdaa l quraa yaħmilu hadaayaa li l laðiina yataɛallamuuna fii haaðihi l madaarisi l lay-liyyati taʃjiiɛan lahum fa jtamaɛa l fallaaħuuna ħaw-lahu fa daɛaa l mufattiʃu mraʔatan minhum wa ṭalaba minhaa ʔan taqraʔa kalimatan ʔaʃaara ʔilayhaa fii ki-taabin kaana fii yadihi. fa qaraʔat bi ṣawtin ɛaalin: 'mindiilun.' fa qaala lahaa: 'ʔaħsanti.' wa ʔaɛ-ṭaahaa mindiilan. θumma daɛaa rajulan wɛ ṭalaba min-hu ʔan yaqraʔa kalimatan ʔaʃaara ʔilayhaa. fa qaraʔa bi surɛatin: 'θawrun.' wa kaanat i l kalimatu ʃay-ʔan ʔaaxara. fa qaala lahu l mufattiʃu: 'ʔunður jayyidan wa qraʔ.' fa naðara l rajulu marratan ʔux-raa wa qaala: 'θawrun.' fa qaamat zawjatuhu wa qaa-lat: 'zawjii yuħsinu l qiraaʔata walaakinnahu fii ħaajatin ʃadiidatin ʔilaa θawrin yaħruθu bihi l ʔarḍa.'

-oOo-

Local News

9.(a)

أخبار محلية

القدس — لما اقترب السيد ف من أحد
شبابيك داره رأى أن سيارته الواقفة
أمام البيت قد رفعت استعدادا لأخذ
إطاراتها فأخبر في الحال مركز البوليس
بذلك فخف رجال البوليس إلى مكان
الحادث ولكنهم لم يعثروا على أحد
بقرب السيارة ولا يزال التحقيق مستمرا

(b)

(أخبار محلية)

القدس — لما اقترب السيد ف من أحد شبابيك داره
رأى أن سيارته الواقفة أمام البيت قد رفعت استعدادا
لأخذ إطاراتها فأخبر في الحال مركز البوليس بذلك فخف رجال
البوليس إلى مكان الحادث ولكنهم لم يعثروا على أحد بقرب

السيارة ولا يزال التحقيق مستمرا

(c)

[ʔaxbaarun maħalliyyatun]

ʔal qudsu:- lammaa qtaraba l sayyidu [faaʔ] min ʔaħadi ʃabaabiiki daarihi raʔaa ʔanna sayyaaratahu l waaqifata ʔamaama l bayti qad rufiɛat i stiɛdaadan li ʔaxði ʔiṭaaraatihaa. fa ʔaxbara fii l ħaali markaza l buuliisi bi ðaalika. fa xaffa rijaalu l buuliisi ʔilaa makaani l ħaadiθi. walaakinnahum lam yaɛθuruu ɛalaa ʔaħadin bi qurbi l sayyaarati. wa laa yazaalu l taħqiiqu mustamirran.

-oOo-

10.(a) Cairo News Agency.

القاهرة - وكالة الأنباء العربية -

ستبدأ شركة الطيران اللبنانية عملها في

أواخر هذا الشهر المقبل وقد اشترت

ثلاث عشرة طائرة تجارية من بريطانيا

وخمس طائرات من أمريكا لنقل الركاب

بين لبنان والأقطار العربية وستعقد

الشركة اتفاقيات مع شركات الطيران

الأمريكية والبريطانية لنقل ركابها إلى

أوربا وأمريكا وبالعكس وهناك عدة

شركات لبنانية للطيران تم لها الحصول

على الترخيص وهي الآن تعمل على إيجاد

الطائرات المطلوبة لها

(b)

القاهرة - وكالة الأنباء العربية - ستبدأ شركة الطيران
اللبنانية عملها في أواخر هذا الشهر المقبل وقد اشترت ثلاث
عشرة طائرة تجارية من بريطانيا وخمس طائرات من أمريكا لنقل
الركاب بين لبنان والأقطار العربية وستعقد الشركة
اتفاقيات مع شركات الطيران الأمريكية والبريطانية لنقل
ركابها إلى أوربا وأمريكا وبالعكس وهنالك عدة شركات لبنانية
للطيران تم لها الحصول على الترخيص وهي الآن تعمل على
إيجاد الطائرات المطلوبة لها

(c)

ʕal qaahiratu: wikaalatu l ʕanbaaʕi l ɛarabiyyati - satabdaʕu ʃarikatu l ṭayaraani l lubnaaniyyatu ɛamalahaa fii ʕawaaxiri haaðaa l ʃahri l muqbili wa qad i ʃtarat θalaaθa ɛaʃarata ṭaaʕiratan tijaariyyatan min biriṭaaniyaa wa xamsa ṭaaʕiraatin min ʕamriikaa li naqli l rukkaabi bayna lubnaana wa l ʕaqṭaari l ɛarabiyyati wa sataɛqidu l ʃarikatu ttifaaqiyyaatin maɛa ʃarikaati l ṭayaraani l ʕamriikiyyati wa l biriṭaaniyyati li naqli rukkaabihaa ʕilaa ʕuurubbaa wa ʕamriikaa wa bi l ɛaksi. wa hunaaka ɛiddatu ʃarikaatin lubnaaniyyatin li l ṭayaraani tamma lahaa l ħuṣuulu ɛalaa l tarxiiṣi wa hiya l ʕaana taɛmalu fii ʕiijaadi l ṭaaʕiraati l maṭluubati lahaa.

-oOo-

APPENDIX B

The frequent need for speed together with a natural tendency towards economy of effort tend to produce irregularities in th cursive rendering of the Arabic script. Persian and, from Persian, Urdu, have evolved a system from such anomalies, and instituted a recognised style having its own discipline and artistic effects; this is the Persian "Shikaste" and Urdu "Shikasta"[1] or "broken" style. The most striking characteristic of this "running hand" is that the separate letters are almost invariably joined to a followin letter, but "oddities" of letter- and word-shape occur throughout.

These "irregularities" are found, too, in Arabic. They are, however, to be considered, not as systematic within a new style but as peculiarities which the student should be able to recognise but which he should not imitate at least in the early stages. Some examples[2] are given below together with their "orthodox" and transcribed forms; some - for example, No.45 - are clear attempts at Persian Shikaste; some are still in current use, while others are outmoded; others again simply illustrate a mixture of styles.

1.	علی تلك	على تلك	[ɛalaa tilka]
2.	سرور الهاشم	سرور الهاشم	[suruuru l haaʃimi]
3.	بضنك	بضنك	[bi ḍanki]
4.	الشظف	الشظف	[ʔal ʃaðafu]
5.	الساعة	الساعة	[ʔal saaɛatu]

---

1. The student who reads Urdu may refer to Mr. M. A. Khan Haidari's URDU MANUSCRIPT.

2. The examples have been selected from Louis Cheikho's SPÉCIMENS D'ÉCRITURES ARABES POUR LA LECTURE DES MANUSCRITS ANCIENS ET MODERNE

6.	كما وصفتموها	كما وصفتموها	[kamaa waṣaftumuuhaa]
7.	هي	هي	[hiya]
8.	الفريدة	الفريدة	[ʕal fariidatu]
9.	هذه	هذه	[haaðihi]
10.	أقول	أقول	[ʕaquulu]
11.	ضميرك	ضميرك	[ḍamiiruka]
12.	بقاك	بقاك	[baqaaka]
13.	العيون	العيون	[ʕal ɛuyuunu]
14.	من	من	[man]
15.	الفضائل	الفضائل	[ʕal faḍaaʕilu]
16.	بكائي	بكائي	[bukaaʕii]
17.	ابرهيم	ابراهيم	[ʕibraahiimu]
18.	الوضيع	الوضيع	[ʕal waḍiiɛu]
19.	وتجله	وتجله	[wa tujilluhu]
20.	لجماله	لجماله	[li jamaalihi]
21.	لمنظره [1]	لمنظره	[li manðarihi]

1. This irregularity is very common.

22.	الكرامة [1]	الكرامة		[ʕal karaamatu]
23.	عن البشر	عن البشر		[ɛan i l baʃari]
24.	الهوان	الهوان		[ʕal hawaanu]
25.	سلموا	سلموا		[sullimuu]
26.	الآخرين	الآخرين		[ʕal ʕaaxariina]
27.	وبخ	وبخ		[wabbix]
28.	الخطاة	الخطاة		[ʕal xuţaatu]
29.	الخواجة	الخواجة		[ʕal xawaajatu]
30.	جبرايل	جبرايل		[jibraayiil]
31.	مسرورين	مسرورين		[masruuriina]
32.	للدوام	لدوام		[li dawaami]
33.	ليوم ٧ [2]	ليوم ٧		[li yawmi.....]
34.		كما		[kamaa]
35.	يقولون	يقولون		[yaquuluuna]
36.	حواصلها	حواصلها		[ħawaaşiluhaa]
37.	الطالب	الطالب		[ʕal ţaalibu]

1. This irregularity is very common.
2. An example of a merchant's "shorthand".

38.	من	من	[man]
39.	السؤال	السؤال	[ʕal suʕaalu]
40.	وما	وما	[wa maa]
41.	لجنابكم	لجنابكم	[li janaabikum]
42.	الجاهل	الجاهل	[ʕal jaahilu]
43.	الاخ الاجل الامجد	الأخ الأجل الأمجد	[ʕal axu l ʕajallu l ʕamjadu]
44.	بهذا	بهذا	[bi haaðaa]

APPENDIX C

Some Relevant Terminology

أسماء حروف الهجاء	ʕasmaaʕu ħuruufi l hijaaʕi	the names of the letters of the alphabet.
الحروف المفتوحة	ʕal ħuruufu l maftuuħatu	letters with fatħah.
الحروف المكسورة	ʕal ħuruufu l maksuuratu	letters with kasrah.
الحروف المضمومة	ʕal ħuruufu l maḍmuumatu	letters with ḍammah.
الحروف الساكنة	ʕal ħuruufu l saakinatu	letters with sukuun.
الحروف المسكنة	ʕal ħuruufu l musakkanatu	
الحروف المشددة المفتوحة	ʕal ħuruufu l muʃaddadatu l maftuuħatu	letters with taʃdiid and sukuun.
كتابة	kitaabatun	writing.
خط	xaṭṭun	calligraphy; calligraphic style; line.
خطاط	xaṭṭaaṭun	calligrapher.
رسم الحروف	rasmu l ħuruufi	calligraphic art.
صورة	ṣuuratun	form, shape; appearance.
شكل	ʃaklun	
هيئة	hayʕatun	
نقطة	nuqṭatun	dot.
قلم قصب	qalamu qaṣabin	reed-pen.
طرف القلم	ṭarafu l qalami	nib [of reed-pen].
قطة القلم	qaṭṭatu l qalami	
شحمة (القلم)	ʃaħmatu [l qalami]	lit. 'the fat [of the pen', i.e. the white interior of the reed contrasted with the exterior. Comparison is with the fat and lean of meat.

لحمة (القلم)		laħmatu [l qalami]	lit. 'the flesh [of the pen]', i.e. the reddish exterior of the reed.
			The four stages (أركان [ʕarkaanun], lit. 'supports') in cutting the nib:-
فتح	(i)	fatħun	(i) opening.
نحت	(ii)	naħtun	(ii) trimming.
شق	(iii)	ʃaqqun	(iii) splitting [to facilitate retention of ink.
قط	(iv)	qaṭṭun	(iv) [the final cross-] cut.
سن		sinnun	nib [metal]; tooth [e.g. of س].
وصل الحروف		waṣlu l ħuruufi	the joining of letters.
في بداية (الكلمة)		fii bidaayati [l kalimati]	initial [in a word].
في وسط (الكلمة)		fii wasṭi [l kalimati]	medial [in a word].
في نهاية (الكلمة)		fii nihaayati [l kalimati]	final [in a word].
مفرد		mufrad	separate.
منفرد		munfarid	
كلمات تكتب بشكل خاص		kalimaatun tuktabu bi ʃaklin xaaṣṣin	words written in a special form, e.g. archaisms.
حذف الألف		ħaδfu l ʕalifi	the omission of ʕalif, e.g. in هذا [haaδaa].
شرطة		ʃarṭatun	stroke.
خط أفقي		xaṭṭun ʕufqiyyun	horizontal line.
منسطح		munsaṭiħun	straight, horizontal, [of stroke].
خط رأسي		xaṭṭun raʕsiyyun	vertical line.
خط عمودي		xaṭṭun ɛamuudii	
منتصب		muntaṣibun	upright, vertical, [of stroke].

مستقيم	mustaqiimun	straight.
منحن	munħanin	curved.
منحدر	munħadirun	sloping.
مائل	maaʔilun	
مستدق	mustadiqqun	tapering.
منكب	munkabbun	descending from left to right, e.g. first stroke of بر.
مستلق	mustalqin	descending from right to left, e.g. ر .
مستدير	mustadiirun	rounded [as lower half of ع].
عمق	ɛumqun	depth.
ارتفاع	ʔirtifaaɛun	height.
عرض	ɛarḍun	width.
زاوية	zaawiyatun	angle.
صندوق	ṣunduuqun	loop, lit. 'box', as of ص .
حلقة	ħalaqatun	loop, lit. 'ring', as of ف.
قنطرة	qanṭaratun	bridge, e.g. t + m تم .
ذيل	ðaylun	tail, [as of ع].
رقبة	raqabatun	neck, [as of كف].
مطموسة	maṭmuusatun	blocked [of medial ع].
مفتوحة	maftuuħatun	open, unblocked [as of medial ـهـ].
كاسة	kaasatun	lit. 'wine-glass'. Refers to final semicircular component of س , ص.

التعريق	ʕal taɛriiqu	The inclusion of the final semi-circular component of س , ش , ص , ض .
معرق	muɛarraqun	س, ش, ص or ض having the final curvature, i.e. final or isolated س , etc.
(السين) غير المعرقة	[ʕal siinu] ɣayru l muɛarraqati	initial or medial [siin].
الهاء المشقوقة	ʕal haaʕu l maʃ-quuqatu	lit. ‘split haaʕ’, i.e. هـ .

The following terms are current for punctuation marks in modern texts:

الترقيم	ʕal tarqiimu	punctuation.
علامات الترقيم	ɛalaamaatu l tar-qiimi	punctuation marks.
فاصلة	faaṣilatun	comma.
قاطعة	qaaṭiɛatun	full stop.
فاصلة كبرى	faaṣilatun kubraa	semi-colon.
شارحة	ʃaariḥatun	colon.
علامة الاستفهام	ɛalaamatu l istifhaami	question-mark.
علامة التعجب	ɛalaamatu l taɛajjubi	exclamation-mark.
قوس	qawsun	inverted commas [lit. ‘arch’].
افتح قوسا	ʕiftaḥ qawsan	inverted commas on!
اقفل القوس	ʕiqfil i l qawsa	inverted commas off!
علامات التنصيص	ɛalaamaatu l tanṣiiṣi	quotation marks, inverted commas.

APPENDIX D.

Ready-Reference Tables.

In the following eleven ready-reference tables[1] which summarise two- and three-letter combinations, the initial form of a letter is to be found opposite the appropriate symbol in the vertical column on the extreme right of each table; final shapes are found by reference to the symbols of the horizontal "axis" at the top. Thus, to refer to the two-letter combination jiim + raaʕ, turn to Table 1 which shows all two-letter combinations, look first for the shape ج on the right of the table, then read across to the vertical column illustrating final ـر . The remaining ten tables are constructed in the same manner as far as initial and final shapes are concerned, but each table illustrates throughout a given medial shape. The medial shape of a given table is indicated by the number in the top right hand corner in accordance with the following key:

(1. Two-letter combinations.)

Three-letter combinations:

2. Medial baaʕ, taaʕ, θaaʕ, nuun, yaaʕ.
3. " jiim, ħaaʕ, xaaʕ.
4. " siin, ʃiin.
5. " ṣaad, ḍaad.
6. " ṭaaʕ, ðaaʕ.
7. " ɛayn, ɣayn.
8. " faaʕ, qaaf.
9. " kaaf, laam.
10. " miim.
11. " haaʕ.

Thus, to find faaʕ + ɛayn + laam, refer to Table 7, then to the symbol ف on the right, and read across to the vertical column under ل .

The separate letters are not especially illustrated; their isolated forms appear in the horizontal "axis" and their final forms in the appropriate vertical columns.

---

1. The idea of the tables was originally suggested to me by tables in the Persian Nastaɛliq style made by a Persian calligrapher for Mr. P.A.D.MacCarthy. [footnote continued overleaf]

Except for isolated and final ف - which provide the only example of a dot which is not used to distinguish a letter in Arabic- dots are omitted throughout. In the vertical "axis", the shape ٮ = baaʕ, taaʕ, θaaʕ, nuun and yaaʕ, since dots alone distinguish these letters in initial form; ح = jiim, ħaaʕ, xaaʕ; ف = faaʕ, qaaf, etc. ل = both kaaf and laam since in the great majority of contexts, the "handle" of kaaf is the sole difference between them. Similarly, it has not been considered necessary to include a separate table showing medial laam.[1]

Variants are not included in the tables. This applies particularly to final ʃiin, ḍaad, nuun and haaʕ.[2,3].

It should be realised by the student that this is essentially a practical book designed to help him to improve his writing of the Arabic script. The tables are not strictly linguistic, since they include patterns which are inoperative in the language. The student will come to recognise the impossibility of certain junctions of the gutturals, emphatics, liquids, velars, etc., as he progresses to a greater knowledge of the phonological structure of Arabic. Thus, for example, on Table 7, the horizontal column opposite the initial shape ع is, linguistically speaking, "nonsense", but has perhaps some value for the art of writing the letter-shapes. Even more obvious "impossibilities" are those examples which show the junction of the same letter, initial, medial and final, e.g. kaaf + kaaf + kaaf.

ERRATUM

The symbols of the horizontal "axis" follow the order of the Arabic alphabet. و and ه , however, are in incorrect order throughout the tables.

[continuation of footnote 1 on previous page]

It is possible--and profitable--to construct similar tables for the learning of any calligraphic style.

1. The shapes shown are not operative for laam before ʕalif, kaaf and laam. See Chapter IX, pp.87-92.
2. The shape ه has been used throughout for final haaʕ: remember that the junction of initial ع with final ه of the shape ـه has a different implication as to the shape of ع.
3. It is convenient to note here that the junction initial faaʕ/qaaf and final yaaʕ, shown in Table 1 as في, is more usually rendered في .

2	ا	ٮ	ح	د	ر	س	ص	ط	ع	ف	ٯ	ك	ل	م	ں	و	ه	ى
ٮ	ٮا	ٮٮ	ٮح	ٮد	ٮر	ٮس	ٮص	ٮط	ٮع	ٮف	ٮٯ	ٮك	ٮل	ٮم	ٮں	ٮو	ٮه	ٮى
ح	حا	حٮ	حح	حد	حر	حس	حص	حط	حع	حف	حٯ	حك	حل	حم	حں	حو	حه	حى
س	سا	سٮ	سح	سد	سر	سس	سص	سط	سع	سف	سٯ	سك	سل	سم	سں	سو	سه	سى
ص	صا	صٮ	صح	صد	صر	صس	صص	صط	صع	صف	صٯ	صك	صل	صم	صں	صو	صه	صى
ط	طا	طٮ	طح	طد	طر	طس	طص	طط	طع	طف	طٯ	طك	طل	طم	طں	طو	طه	طى
ع	عا	عٮ	عح	عد	عر	عس	عص	عط	عع	عف	عٯ	عك	عل	عم	عں	عو	عه	عى
ف	فا	فٮ	فح	فد	فر	فس	فص	فط	فع	فف	فٯ	فك	فل	فم	فں	فو	فه	فى
ك	كا	كٮ	كح	كد	كر	كس	كص	كط	كع	كف	كٯ	كك	كل	كم	كں	كو	كه	كى
م	ما	مٮ	مح	مد	مر	مس	مص	مط	مع	مف	مٯ	مك	مل	مم	مں	مو	مه	مى
ه	ها	هٮ	هح	هد	هر	هس	هص	هط	هع	هف	هٯ	هك	هل	هم	هں	هو	هه	هى

+	ا	ٮ	ح	د	ر	س	ص	ط	ع	ڡ	ٯ	ك	ل	م	ہ	و	ه	ى
ٮ	ٮا	ٮٮ	ٮح	ٮد	ٮر	ٮس	ٮص	ٮط	ٮع	ٮڡ	ٮٯ	ٮك	ٮل	ٮم	ٮہ	ٮو	ٮه	ٮى
ح	حا	حٮ	حح	حد	حر	حس	حص	حط	حع	حڡ	حٯ	حك	حل	حم	حہ	حو	حه	حى
س	سا	سٮ	سح	سد	سر	سس	سص	سط	سع	سڡ	سٯ	سك	سل	سم	سہ	سو	سه	سى
ص	صا	صٮ	صح	صد	صر	صس	صص	صط	صع	صڡ	صٯ	صك	صل	صم	صہ	صو	صه	صى
ط	طا	طٮ	طح	طد	طر	طس	طص	طط	طع	طڡ	طٯ	طك	طل	طم	طہ	طو	طه	طى
ع	عا	عٮ	عح	عد	عر	عس	عص	عط	عع	عڡ	عٯ	عك	عل	عم	عہ	عو	عه	عى
ڡ	ڡا	ڡٮ	ڡح	ڡد	ڡر	ڡس	ڡص	ڡط	ڡع	ڡڡ	ڡٯ	ڡك	ڡل	ڡم	ڡہ	ڡو	ڡه	ڡى
ك	كا	كٮ	كح	كد	كر	كس	كص	كط	كع	كڡ	كٯ	كك	كل	كم	كہ	كو	كه	كى
م	ما	مٮ	مح	مد	مر	مس	مص	مط	مع	مڡ	مٯ	مك	مل	مم	مہ	مو	مه	مى
ه	ها	هٮ	هح	هد	هر	هس	هص	هط	هع	هڡ	هٯ	هك	هل	هم	هہ	هو	هه	هى

5	ا	ب	ح	د	ر	س	ص	ط	ع	ف	ق	ك	ل	م	ن	و	ه	ى
ب	بصا	بصب	بصح	بصد	بصر	بصس	بصص	بصط	بصع	بصف	بصق	بصك	بصل	بصم	بصن	بصو	بصه	بصى
ح	حصا	حصب	حصح	حصد	حصر	حصس	حصص	حصط	حصع	حصف	حصق	حصك	حصل	حصم	حصن	حصو	حصه	حصى
س	سصا	سصب	سصح	سصد	سصر	سصس	سصص	سصط	سصع	سصف	سصق	سصك	سصل	سصم	سصن	سصو	سصه	سصى
ص	صصا	صصب	صصح	صصد	صصر	صصس	صصص	صصط	صصع	صصف	صصق	صصك	صصل	صصم	صصن	صصو	صصه	صصى
ط	طصا	طصب	طصح	طصد	طصر	طصس	طصص	طصط	طصع	طصف	طصق	طصك	طصل	طصم	طصن	طصو	طصه	طصى
ع	عصا	عصب	عصح	عصد	عصر	عصس	عصص	عصط	عصع	عصف	عصق	عصك	عصل	عصم	عصن	عصو	عصه	عصى
ف	فصا	فصب	فصح	فصد	فصر	فصس	فصص	فصط	فصع	فصف	فصق	فصك	فصل	فصم	فصن	فصو	فصه	فصى
ك	كصا	كصب	كصح	كصد	كصر	كصس	كصص	كصط	كصع	كصف	كصق	كصك	كصل	كصم	كصن	كصو	كصه	كصى
م	مصا	مصب	مصح	مصد	مصر	مصس	مصص	مصط	مصع	مصف	مصق	مصك	مصل	مصم	مصن	مصو	مصه	مصى
ه	هصا	هصب	هصح	هصد	هصر	هصس	هصص	هصط	هصع	هصف	هصق	هصك	هصل	هصم	هصن	هصو	هصه	هصى

6	ا	ٮ	ح	د	ر	س	ص	ط	ع	ف	ٯ	ك	ل	م	ں	و	ه	ى
ٮ	ٮطا	ٮطٮ	ٮطح	ٮطد	ٮطر	ٮطس	ٮطص	ٮطط	ٮطع	ٮطف	ٮطٯ	ٮطك	ٮطل	ٮطم	ٮطں	ٮطو	ٮطه	ٮطى
ح	حطا	حطٮ	حطح	حطد	حطر	حطس	حطص	حطط	حطع	حطف	حطٯ	حطك	حطل	حطم	حطں	حطو	حطه	حطى
س	سطا	سطٮ	سطح	سطد	سطر	سطس	سطص	سطط	سطع	سطف	سطٯ	سطك	سطل	سطم	سطں	سطو	سطه	سطى
ص	صطا	صطٮ	صطح	صطد	صطر	صطس	صطص	صطط	صطع	صطف	صطٯ	صطك	صطل	صطم	صطں	صطو	صطه	صطى
ط	ططا	ططٮ	ططح	ططد	ططر	ططس	ططص	ططط	ططع	ططف	ططٯ	ططك	ططل	ططم	ططں	ططو	ططه	ططى
ع	عطا	عطٮ	عطح	عطد	عطر	عطس	عطص	عطط	عطع	عطف	عطٯ	عطك	عطل	عطم	عطں	عطو	عطه	عطى
ف	فطا	فطٮ	فطح	فطد	فطر	فطس	فطص	فطط	فطع	فطف	فطٯ	فطك	فطل	فطم	فطں	فطو	فطه	فطى
ك	كطا	كطٮ	كطح	كطد	كطر	كطس	كطص	كطط	كطع	كطف	كطٯ	كطك	كطل	كطم	كطں	كطو	كطه	كطى
م	مطا	مطٮ	مطح	مطد	مطر	مطس	مطص	مطط	مطع	مطف	مطٯ	مطك	مطل	مطم	مطں	مطو	مطه	مطى
ه	هطا	هطٮ	هطح	هطد	هطر	هطس	هطص	هطط	هطع	هطف	هطٯ	هطك	هطل	هطم	هطں	هطو	هطه	هطى

7	ا	ٮ	ح	د	ر	س	ص	ط	ع	ف	ٯ	ك	ل	م	ﻪ	و	ه	ى
ٮ	ٮما	ٮمٮ	ٮمح	ٮمد	ٮمر	ٮمس	ٮمص	ٮمط	ٮمع	ٮمف	ٮمٯ	ٮمك	ٮمل	ٮمم	ٮمﻪ	ٮمو	ٮمه	ٮمى
ح	حما	حمٮ	حمح	حمد	حمر	حمس	حمص	حمط	حمع	حمف	حمٯ	حمك	حمل	حمم	حمﻪ	حمو	حمه	حمى
س	سما	سمٮ	سمح	سمد	سمر	سمس	سمص	سمط	سمع	سمف	سمٯ	سمك	سمل	سمم	سمﻪ	سمو	سمه	سمى
ص	صما	صمٮ	صمح	صمد	صمر	صمس	صمص	صمط	صمع	صمف	صمٯ	صمك	صمل	صمم	صمﻪ	صمو	صمه	صمى
ط	طما	طمٮ	طمح	طمد	طمر	طمس	طمص	طمط	طمع	طمف	طمٯ	طمك	طمل	طمم	طمﻪ	طمو	طمه	طمى
ع	عما	عمٮ	عمح	عمد	عمر	عمس	عمص	عمط	عمع	عمف	عمٯ	عمك	عمل	عمم	عمﻪ	عمو	عمه	عمى
ف	فما	فمٮ	فمح	فمد	فمر	فمس	فمص	فمط	فمع	فمف	فمٯ	فمك	فمل	فمم	فمﻪ	فمو	فمه	فمى
ك	كما	كمٮ	كمح	كمد	كمر	كمس	كمص	كمط	كمع	كمف	كمٯ	كمك	كمل	كمم	كمﻪ	كمو	كمه	كمى
م	مما	ممٮ	ممح	ممد	ممر	ممس	ممص	ممط	ممع	ممف	ممٯ	ممك	ممل	ممم	ممﻪ	ممو	ممه	ممى
ه	هما	همٮ	همح	همد	همر	همس	همص	همط	همع	همف	همٯ	همك	همل	همم	همﻪ	همو	همه	همى

ى	ه	و	ں	م	ل	ك	ٯ	ف	ع	ط	ص	س	ر	د	ح	ٮ	ا	8
ٮعى	ٮعه	ٮعو	ٮعں	ٮعم	ٮعل	ٮعك	ٮعٯ	ٮعف	ٮعع	ٮعط	ٮعص	ٮعس	ٮعر	ٮعد	ٮعح	ٮعٮ	ٮعا	ٮ
حعى	حعه	حعو	حعں	حعم	حعل	حعك	حعٯ	حعف	حعع	حعط	حعص	حعس	حعر	حعد	حعح	حعٮ	حعا	ح
سعى	سعه	سعو	سعں	سعم	سعل	سعك	سعٯ	سعف	سعع	سعط	سعص	سعس	سعر	سعد	سعح	سعٮ	سعا	س
صعى	صعه	صعو	صعں	صعم	صعل	صعك	صعٯ	صعف	صعع	صعط	صعص	صعس	صعر	صعد	صعح	صعٮ	صعا	ص
طعى	طعه	طعو	طعں	طعم	طعل	طعك	طعٯ	طعف	طعع	طعط	طعص	طعس	طعر	طعد	طعح	طعٮ	طعا	ط
ععى	ععه	ععو	ععں	ععم	ععل	ععك	ععٯ	ععف	ععع	ععط	ععص	ععس	ععر	ععد	ععح	ععٮ	ععا	ع
فعى	فعه	فعو	فعں	فعم	فعل	فعك	فعٯ	فعف	فعع	فعط	فعص	فعس	فعر	فعد	فعح	فعٮ	فعا	ف
كعى	كعه	كعو	كعں	كعم	كعل	كعك	كعٯ	كعف	كعع	كعط	كعص	كعس	كعر	كعد	كعح	كعٮ	كعا	ك
معى	معه	معو	معں	معم	معل	معك	معٯ	معف	معع	معط	معص	معس	معر	معد	معح	معٮ	معا	م
هعى	هعه	هعو	هعں	هعم	هعل	هعك	هعٯ	هعف	هعع	هعط	هعص	هعس	هعر	هعد	هعح	هعٮ	هعا	ه

٩	ا	ٮ	ح	د	ر	س	ص	ط	ع	ف	ٯ	ك	ل	م	ہ	و	ه	ى
ٮ	ٮكا	ٮكٮ	ٮكح	ٮكد	ٮكر	ٮكس	ٮكص	ٮكط	ٮكع	ٮكف	ٮكٯ	ٮكك	ٮكل	ٮكم	ٮكہ	ٮكو	ٮكه	ٮكى
ح	حكا	حكٮ	حكح	حكد	حكر	حكس	حكص	حكط	حكع	حكف	حكٯ	حكك	حكل	حكم	حكہ	حكو	حكه	حكى
س	سكا	سكٮ	سكح	سكد	سكر	سكس	سكص	سكط	سكع	سكف	سكٯ	سكك	سكل	سكم	سكہ	سكو	سكه	سكى
ص	صكا	صكٮ	صكح	صكد	صكر	صكس	صكص	صكط	صكع	صكف	صكٯ	صكك	صكل	صكم	صكہ	صكو	صكه	صكى
ط	طكا	طكٮ	طكح	طكد	طكر	طكس	طكص	طكط	طكع	طكف	طكٯ	طكك	طكل	طكم	طكہ	طكو	طكه	طكى
ع	عكا	عكٮ	عكح	عكد	عكر	عكس	عكص	عكط	عكع	عكف	عكٯ	عكك	عكل	عكم	عكہ	عكو	عكه	عكى
ف	فكا	فكٮ	فكح	فكد	فكر	فكس	فكص	فكط	فكع	فكف	فكٯ	فكك	فكل	فكم	فكہ	فكو	فكه	فكى
ك	ككا	ككٮ	ككح	ككد	ككر	ككس	ككص	ككط	ككع	ككف	ككٯ	ككك	ككل	ككم	ككہ	ككو	ككه	ككى
م	مكا	مكٮ	مكح	مكد	مكر	مكس	مكص	مكط	مكع	مكف	مكٯ	مكك	مكل	مكم	مكہ	مكو	مكه	مكى
ه	هكا	هكٮ	هكح	هكد	هكر	هكس	هكص	هكط	هكع	هكف	هكٯ	هكك	هكل	هكم	هكہ	هكو	هكه	هكى

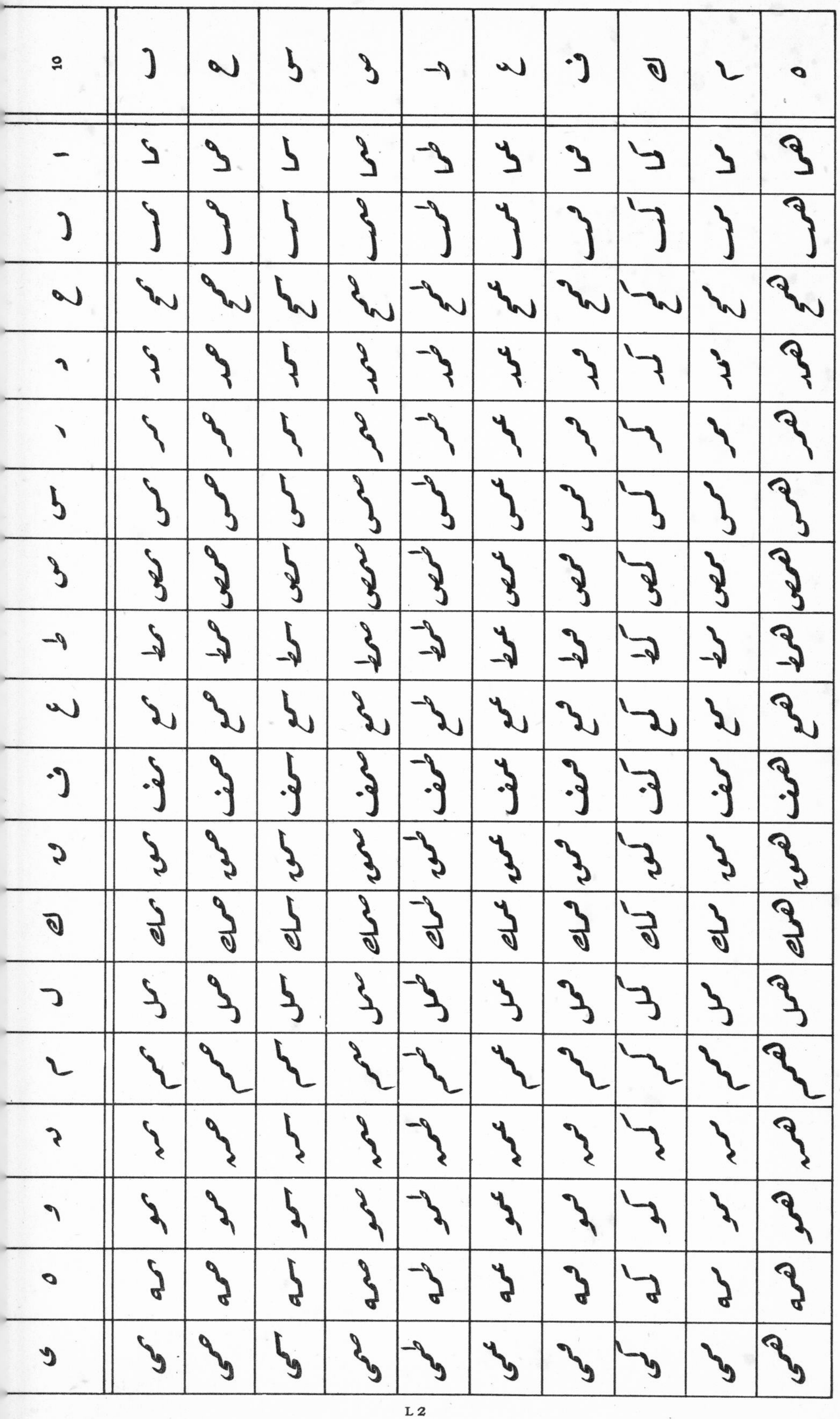

11	ا	ٮ	ح	د	ر	س	ص	ط	ع	ف	ٯ	ك	ل	م	ں	و	ه	ى
ٮ	ٮها	ٮهٮ	ٮهح	ٮهد	ٮهر	ٮهس	ٮهص	ٮهط	ٮهع	ٮهف	ٮهٯ	ٮهك	ٮهل	ٮهم	ٮهں	ٮهو	ٮهه	ٮهى
ح	حها	حهٮ	حهح	حهد	حهر	حهس	حهص	حهط	حهع	حهف	حهٯ	حهك	حهل	حهم	حهں	حهو	حهه	حهى
س	سها	سهٮ	سهح	سهد	سهر	سهس	سهص	سهط	سهع	سهف	سهٯ	سهك	سهل	سهم	سهں	سهو	سهه	سهى
ص	صها	صهٮ	صهح	صهد	صهر	صهس	صهص	صهط	صهع	صهف	صهٯ	صهك	صهل	صهم	صهں	صهو	صهه	صهى
ط	طها	طهٮ	طهح	طهد	طهر	طهس	طهص	طهط	طهع	طهف	طهٯ	طهك	طهل	طهم	طهں	طهو	طهه	طهى
ع	عها	عهٮ	عهح	عهد	عهر	عهس	عهص	عهط	عهع	عهف	عهٯ	عهك	عهل	عهم	عهں	عهو	عهه	عهى
ف	فها	فهٮ	فهح	فهد	فهر	فهس	فهص	فهط	فهع	فهف	فهٯ	فهك	فهل	فهم	فهں	فهو	فهه	فهى
ك	كها	كهٮ	كهح	كهد	كهر	كهس	كهص	كهط	كهع	كهف	كهٯ	كهك	كهل	كهم	كهں	كهو	كهه	كهى
م	مها	مهٮ	مهح	مهد	مهر	مهس	مهص	مهط	مهع	مهف	مهٯ	مهك	مهل	مهم	مهں	مهو	مهه	مهى
ه	هها	ههٮ	ههح	ههد	ههر	ههس	ههص	ههط	ههع	ههف	ههٯ	ههك	ههل	ههم	ههں	ههو	ههه	ههى

APPENDIX E

Translation of Examples

Translations in the present appendix, which has been included as a ready-reference for the beginner, are summary and too often only approximate. They are primarily intended to enable the student to identify the Arabic word. Verbal forms are all translated by the English infinitival form with "to" irrespective of Arabic tense, mood, person, etc. The latter categories are indicated by the bracketed abbreviations;[1] where there is no accompanying bracket, the Arabic verbal form is that of the 3rd person singular masculine of the perfect tense.

The student should note that in order to illustrate letter-combinations fully, it has been necessary to use word-material of very mixed character: thus rare Classical words as بهس (II,2,18) appear in association with as modern a word as بيرة (II,3,4). The great majority of the words, however, are still in current use. Rarer words are marked with an asterisk.

I.

1. 1. to permit. 2. son. 3. mother.
4. not to degrade oneself. (3 s.m.impf.) 5. to announce. 6. to grow up. (3 s.m.juss.)
7. problem; matter. 8. to ask (3 s.m.impf.) 9. to ask.
10. woman. 11. courage, strength. 12. to be acquainted with. (3 s.m.juss.)

2. 1. to stand. 2. shame. 3. passer-by.
4. youth. 5. to travel, go. 6. to come.

3. 1. to write. (3 p.m.perf.) 2. to write. (3 p.m. subj. and juss.) 3. to be. (3 p.m. subj. and juss.)

---

1. Abbreviations used are: 1/2/3 = 1st/2nd/3rd person; s./p. = singular/plural; m./f. = masculine/feminine; perf./impf./impve./subj./juss. = perfect/imperfect/imperative/subjunctive/jussive; pass. = passive. Other abbreviations are: acc. = accusative, a.p. = active participle, and obl. = oblique case.

4. to write. (p.m. impve.)
5. door (acc.)
6. lion (acc.)
7. king (acc.)
8. thing; matter (acc.)
9. wife (acc.)
10. reward, requital (acc.)
11. right course; true religion.
12. safe
13. he saw him.
14. to get on well with.
15. to frequent.
16. companion.
17. life, existence.
18. alms.
19. Mosaic law.
20. this.
21. that.
22. but, yet.
23. God.
24. Abraham.

II.

2.

1. door; chapter.
2. to dig up.
3. to decide, settle*
4. breast.
5. cold.
6. to charge, attack (3 s.m.impf.)
7. with you (s.m.)
8. pupil.
9. but.
10. where?
11. son.
12. with him.
13. with him.
14. canine tooth.
15. to break out (war).
16. to be acquainted with. (3 s.m.impf.)
17. to thumbprint, stamp.
18. to be delicate of skin; to tune (instrument)*
19. to annul, cancel.
20. tie-ing, binding. (a.p.)
21. to send.
22. to flow (water).
23. to come. (3 s.m.impf.)
24. to become angry*
25. cash, ready money.
26. bug.
27. to charge, attack. (3 s.m.impf.)
28. with you (s.m.)
29. pupil.
30. but.
31. bull.
32. with me.
33. under, down.
34. howling (a.p.)
35. fruit.
36. to be complete.
37. river.
[38. where?]

3.

1. channel, canal.
2. reason, cause.
3. to begin (3 s.m.impf.
4. beer.
5. to sweep.
6. tp take a pinch of.
7. to choose anything clean*
8. to follow.
9. to twist (the foot).
10. to lash, flog*
11. early riser.
12. to be drenched.
13. to explain.
14. year.
15. killed.
16. to open.
17. Panama.
18. to build.

19. house, tent.
20. origin, place of growing.
21. exception.
22. to be clear, understood (3 s.m.subj.)

1. to break an oath.
2. to hide.
3. to attribute (to).
4. to toil.
5. defect.
6. to play.
7. name; title; nickname.
8. to mount.
9. to import; bring.
10. direction.
11. to pant.
12. between, among.
13. we.
14. to be old (3 s.m.impf.)
15. branch.
16. country; native land.
17. about, concerning.
18. art.
19. to be (s.m. impve.)
20. revelation, publication.
21. security.
22. they (f.)
23. with me.
24. inspiration.
25. to forget.
26. regent; trustee.
27. folding.
28. stammering, faltering*
29. in.
30. royal.
31. high.
32. illiterate.
33. she.
34. prohibition.

1. chief.
2. to see (3 s.m. pass.perf.)
3. well.
4. to ask (3 s.m. pass.perf.)
5. growing up (a.p.)
6. to err.
7. sleeping (a.p.)
8. to despair.
9. to see (3 s.m. pass.perf.)
10. looking (a.p., s.f.)
11. monastic cells.
12. to explain.
13. where?
14. house, tent.
15. prince; commander.
16. cups.
17. chief.
18. Palestinian.
19. to build.
20. on.
21. to.

III.

1. to answer.
2. cheese; cowardice.
3. grandmother.
4. corpse; body; figure.
5. to happen.
6. firewood.

7. to make. 8. to be light. 9. right.

10. authority; decree. 11. dispute. 12. to long for.

13. rank; degree; stair. 14. pilgrimage. 15. to flow, run.

16. five. 17. to be ignorant of. 18. rank; degree; stair.

19. spiritual.

<u>3.</u> 1. to erase. 2. wailing. 3. place of pilgrimage.

4. plateau; Najd. 5. slaughter. 6. to feel (3 s.m. impf.)

7. pure, unmixed; typical. 8. to be angry with. 9. to be wholesome (food); efficacious (medicine).

10. sand-hill. 11. touchstone. 12. place.

13. star. 14. we. 15. his brain.

16. grammar; syntax. 17. secret.

<u>4.</u> 1. howling (a.p.) 2. outweighing (a.p.) 3. weaving (a.p.)

4. adviser (a.p.) 5. goring (bull) (a.p.) 6. giving, bestowing (a.p.)

7. to cough. 8. to ask persistently. 9. to forgive.

10. addicted (to).

IV.

<u>1.</u> 1. to go. 2. literature; politeness. 3. to dismiss.

4. to reconcile* 5. to send. 6. light.

<u>2.</u> 1. to give generously. 2. to omit; remove. 3. illustrious.

4. to tell the truth. 5. to make firm, lasting. 6. sweet, palatable.

7. old, ancient. 8. to punch. 9. flexible, supple*

10. diary. 11. this. 12. to create.

13. to flow, run. 14. to steal. 15. to spend.

16. to dismiss. 17. to strengthen. 18. to check.

19. miserly, tight-fisted. 20. to mock.

V.

2. 1. to ask. 2. reason, cause. 3. sadness.

4. to let down (veil, curtain)* 5. to steal. 6. fish-hook.

7. line. 8. slogan; badge. 9. travelling; journey.

10. to doubt. 11. to take by force. 12. to smell (tr.)

13. evidence; certificate. 14. town-wall; house-wall. 15. patient; steady.

16. to endure. 17. to tell the truth. 18. to strike, hit.

19. weakness. 20. row, line. 21. to lose one's way.

22. connection. 23. to melt, liquefy. 24. rightness.

25. to accompany. 26. to determine upon. 27. to consent.

3. 1. to consult. 2. to cause (3 s.m.impf.) 3. to pull out (3 s.m.impf.)

4. envy. 5. undertaking; plan. 6. guard.

7. to line, draw lines on (3 s.m.impf.) 8. busy. 9. to set out (3 s.m.impf.)

10. difficulty, dilemma. 11. to be safe (3 s.m.impf.) 12. the sun.

13. to grow old (3 s.m.impf.) 14. renowned. 15. himself; his soul.

16. to worsen (3 s.m.impf.) 17. to forget. 18. horse.

19. to dye. 20. to lead, walk ahead. 21. to squeeze.

22. to steal. 23. artificial. 24. to suck*

25. small bird; sparrow. 26. instrument of striking. 27. to happen.

28. to steal (3 p.f.perf.)
29. underdone (meat).
30. silver.
31. dispute; enmity.
32. to be eloquent.
33. to thumbprint, stamp.
34. to decide.

<u>4.</u>

1. head.
2. army.
3. to disparage; underestimate.
4. guard.
5. to assault.
6. to cheat.
7. breath.
8. to engrave.
9. to relapse.
10. grave.
11. to bite at.
12. judge.
13. ill.
14. cheap.
15. to urge.
16. to steal.
17. to wriggle.
18. some.
19. to refute; break (promise).
20. to refuse.
21. to retire, draw back.
22. thief.
23. to suck.
24. to lame (of stones entering horse's foot)*

VI.

<u>2.</u>

1. pure.
2. deer.
3. to grind.
4. to make firm; determine upon.
5. adverb; circumstance.
6. to gleam, move about (mirage)*
7. to pierce.
8. to overflow.
9. to remain.
10. to be greedy.
11. to think, suppose.
12. to appear.
13. voluntarily.

<u>3.</u>

1. error.
2. firewood.
3. to flatten.
4. wooden mallet*
5. to look.
6. cleverness, skill.
7. to be fastidious.
8. put out, extinguished.
9. to pronounce,
10. tyrannised.
11. to arrange.
12. to protect; learn by heart (3 p.f.perf.)
13. protection;
14. with self-control.
15. of oil, petroleum.

<u>4.</u>

1. to tie, bind.
2. glance, peep.
3. to be lively, cheerful.
4. to snore (3 s.m.impf.)
5. to protect.
6. to make a mistake.

7. fashion; manner; pattern. 8. folk; clan.

VII.

2. 1. absent. 2. future (noun) 3. deficit; weakness.
4. excuse. 5. purpose. 6. to be twisted (foot, hand).
7. defect; stain; softness. 8. bone. 9. mind; intelligence.
10. opposite. 11. to make a mistake. 12. paternal uncle.
13. about, concerning. 14. wool. 15. swimming.

3. 1. small (p.) 2. to send. 3. meaning.
4. sheep. 5. to be ready, get ready. 6. to plant (3 s.m.impf.)
7. the cheat. 8. to be angry (3 s.m.impf.) 9. to be great (3 s.m.impf.)
10. eagerness. 11. work. 12. mine (explosive).
13. language. 14. swimming. 15. to cancel.

4. 1. eloquent. 2. to shock, frighten. 3. hideous.
4. to be snow-white. 5. to be snow-white. 6. to raise, lift up.
7. to kneel. 8. to reach. 9. to dye, shade*

VIII.

1. 1. middle. 2. rose. 3. to agree.
4. whenever.

2. 1. to smell (good) 2. to learn. 3. dawn.
4. to estimate. 5. to escape. 6. division; destiny.
7. to cut off. 8. to perceive. 9. to sit down.
10. to lock. 11. to think of. 12. pen.
13. worthy. 14. cheetah, leopard. 15. fuel.

3. 1. meeting. 2. to endeavour repeatedly to. 3. to blow (wind).
4. to come (1 p.impf.) 5. report. 6. to disperse (clouds).

7. to shake.
8. only.
9. to do (3 s.m.impf.)
10. wrapped up.
11. to think.
12. the moon.
13. to be accustomed to (3 p.f.perf.)
14. to understand (3 s.m.impf.)
15. shut.
16. forgiven.
17. to find.

4.

1. noble.
2. to tremble.
3. to carry away (wind).
4. to describe.
5. to be merciful to.
6. to be eager for.
7. to stand.
8. to leak.
9. to take an oath.
10. to miss keenly.
11. to be sweetly scented.
12. to crush.
13. to load.
14. to stick to.
15. to burst; crack; crackle*
16. to smite (thunderbolt).
17. to clap.
18. to suspend, hang.
19. to be deep.
20. to oppress.
21. light.
22. to make something good.
23. except.
24. voice.
25. length.
26. busy.
27. people; clan.
28. Lot (proper name).
29. music.

5.

1. to be miserable
2. to edit; compose (3 s.m.impf.)
3. to be miserable (3 m.s.impf.)
4. to take (3 s.m. pass.perf.)
5. to be mean, base.[1]
6. to straighten.
7. repelled.
8. to be black.
9. picture.
10. tall; long.
11. to arrive.
12. or.
13. day.
14. to invite; call (3 p.m.perf.)
15. death.
16. climate, weather.
17. essence; element; gems.
18. to say (3 s.f.impf.)
19. houses, tents.
20. owner; endowed with.
21. without.
22. sunrise; rise (e.g. of Islam)
23. witnesses.

IX.

1.

1. clerk.
2. like a hand.
3. to impose (a task) upon.

---

1. More usually daniʕa.

4. every, each. 5. to write. 6. antimony.

7. lying, lies. 8. panic. 9. profit.

10. like rain. 11. angry. 12. like others (than him).

13. to nurse; guarantee. 14. sleeve. 15. nest; shelter.

16. electrifying (n.) 17. he stitched it. 18. to iron, press.

19. to imitate. 20. no; negative particle. 21. to dress.

22. flesh, meat. 23. flexible* 24. to be necessary.

25. to be eloquent. 26. to stick to. 27. to smack.

28. to play. 29. to attract someone's attention. 30. to punch.

31. when. 32. negative particle. 33. to him.

34. sheet; board. 35. to me.

3\. 1. to complain. 2. coins; ploughshares. 3. to make an example of.

4. to pour. 5. to marry. 6. unfortunate (man).

7. to deny. 8. to relapse. 9. to retire, draw back.

10. to scorn, spurn. 11. to you (m.p.) 12. to enable.

13. he doubted it; it stung him. 14. to complain (1 s.perf.) 15. (particle) without;

16. to overturn. 17. to till (ground); succeed. 18. to imitate.

19. snail. 20. twilight. 21. sincere friend.

22. to make a mistake. 23. to feed (livestock) (tr.) 24. to suspend, hang.

25. perhaps you (m.s.)..... 26. to give reasons for. 27. to teach.

28. publication. 29. perhaps he..... 30. perhaps they (m.) .....

31. to gain advancement (1 s.perf.) 32. high; Proper Name.

4\. 1. with you (s.m.) 2. to rub, scrape. 3. to withhold, keep back; grasp.

4. your (s.m.)
5. your (s.m.) mistake.
6. don't bother! (s.m.)
7. to pour; shed (blood).
8. perhaps you (s.m.).....
9. your (s.m.) paternal uncle.
10. to punish severely.
11. to consent, accept.
12. antimony.
13. to seek mediation.
14. to reach.
15. pound (weight).
16. mule.
17. to transfer.
18. upper part of chest.
19. to do, make.
20. middle-aged.

X.

2.

1. hundred.
2. happy, contented.
3. council, gathering.
4. city.
5. to pass by.
6. to rub; cancel.
7. Egypt.
8. rain.
9. with.
10. open.
11. to be possible.
12. to fill.
13. from which.
14. from, of.
15. craft, occupation.
16. nation.
17. waves.
18. pyramid-shaped.

3.

1. from which.
2. to stand up (1 s.perf.)
3. ugly, foul.
4. to fertilise.
5. dark-skinned.
6. to touch.
7. to buck (e.g. horse).
8. to roast.
9. depth.
10. fish.
11. to put out (the eye)*
12. to poison.
13. fatness.
14. his name.
15. their (m.) name.
16. to call (3 p.m.impf.)
17. my name.

4.

1. standing (a.p.)
2. to be merciful.
3. to divide.
4. to cut off.
5. to smack.
6. mine (explosive).
7. mouth.
8. sleeve.
9. negative particle.
10. they (m.).

XI.

2.

1. bewildered, stupefied (a.p.)
2. suppose he.....
3. to attack.
4. to waste, squander.
5. to spill, pour out.
6. to cut (grass, plants).

7. to squeeze. 8. to rain hard. 9. to flap (intr.); err.

10. thus. 11. interrogative particle. 12. to intend; be anxious about.

13. they (f.). 14. his influence. 15. he.

16. she.

3.

1. to follow. 2. to decorate. 3. and she.

4. with her. 5. to face (1 s.perf.) 6. sleeplessness.

7. to melt, liquefy. 8. foal. 9. to bite at.

10. to rise up. 11. to desire. 12. he pampered you.

13. middle-aged. 14. wool. 15. he pampered him.

16. and he.

4.

1. his god. 2. proof. 3. his courage, strength.

4. story. 5. mistake. 6. rest.

7. rudder. 8. flattening blow. 9. just (s.f.).

10. paternal aunt. 11. he faced him.

XII.

1.

1. to engage servants (3 p.m.impf.) 2. to adopt (child) (3 p.m.impf.) 3. to seek pasturage (3 p.m.impf.)

4. to pretend (3 p.m.impf.) 5. to regard as important (3 p.m.impf.) 6. facing, welcoming (a.p., p.m.)

7. they (m.) will regard as important. 8. Constantinople.

Appendix B.

1. on that (s.f.) 2. the pleasure of the wanderer. 3. with the difficulties of living.

4. the hard life. 5. hour; watch. 6. as you described her.

7. she. 8. the unique (s.f.). 9. this (f.).

10. to say (1 s.impf.) 11. your conscience. 12. your survival.

13. the eyes. 14. who; he who. 15. the virtues.

16. my weeping. 17. Abraham. 18. the humble (man).

19. and she respects him; and you (s.m.) respect him. 20. for his beauty. 21. for his appearance.

22. dignity.
23. about human beings.
24. humility.
25. to hand over (3 p.m.pass. perf.)
26. the others (obl.).
27. to reproach, rebuke (s.m.impve.)
28. the sinners.
29. Mister.....
30. Gabriel.
31. happy people (obl.).
32. for the permanence (of).
33. until the eth day (of).
34. as.
35. to say (3 p.m.impf.)
36. their maws (birds).
37. the student.
38. who, he who.
39. the question.
40. and + negative/relative particle.
41. for your honour.
42. the ignorant.
43. most revered and honoured brother (sc. Dear Sir).
44. with this.

Examples at Appendix A.

1.

Ahmad asked a sailor: "Where did your father die?" The sailor answered: "On a ship he was sailing on the sea." "And when did your grandfather die?" "He, too, died on a ship he was sailing on the sea." "And are you not afraid to sail a ship after that?" Then the sailor said: "Where did your father die?" "In his bed." "And your grandfather?" "In his bed." "And are you not afraid to sleep in a bed after that?"

2.

Two cats found a piece of cheese and took it to the monkey to divide between them. The monkey took the cheese and dividing it into two portions, one of which was larger than the other, put each portion in a pan of his scales. But the larger portion weighed heavier, so he took a little from it with his teeth and ate it, saying: "I want to make it equal to the smaller one." But since he took more than necessary from it, the smaller piece (now) weighed heavier, so he did with the latter what he had done with the former, and continued eating from the heavier of the two portions until he had eaten the whole cheese.

3.

A man opened a fish-shop and above its door hung a small board on which was written: "Fish sold here." One of his friends came and said to him: "Why have you written the word 'here' on the board? Is fish only sold in your shop?" So the shopkeeper erased the word 'here'. Then came a second friend and said to the shopkeeper: "Why have you written the word 'sold' on the board? Do not people understand that you do not distribute fish free of charge?" So he erased the word "sold". Then a third friend came and said: "Why have you written the word 'fish'? Do not people see it and smell it?" So the shopkeeper took down the board.

4.

A king saw an old man planting a palm-tree and said to him: "O Sheikh, do you hope to eat the dates of this palm-tree when it will not bear fruit for many years?" Said the old man: "I am planting the palm so that my grandchildren may eat of its dates just as I myself ate of those my grandfather planted." This pleased the king who gave him twenty dinars which the old man took, saying: "Behold O King, I myself have already eaten of the fruit of this palm." And the king marvelled at his words and gave him a further twenty dinars which the old man took, saying: "O King, the most wondrous thing of all is that the palm has already borne fruit twice this year." And the king was amazed at his words and gave him yet twenty dinars more.

5.

A man once carried to his tent from a nearby forest a bundle of wood which began to weigh heavily upon him. When he tired of carrying it he threw it from his shoulder and called Death down upon him. Death appeared to him and said: "Here I am! Why did you call me?" Said the man: "I called you to load this bundle of wood on my shoulder."

6.

A hunter was hunting and slaughtering sparrows on a cold day and the tears were streaming from his eyes from the extreme cold. One sparrow said to his companion: "Do not fear this man. Don't you see him weeping?" But the other said to him: "Look not at his tears but at what his hands are doing."

7.

A man had a beautiful parrot which knew how to speak, and whenever a man passed by her, she said to him, "Good-day, O my brother." She would go out into the garden in the afternoon and wait for her master to return from his shop, and when she saw him she would say: "Take me home, O my uncle." One day the parrot was missing, and her master was asking everybody about her when a man said to him: "I heard a parrot's voice in my neighbour's house." The parrot's owner went to the man's neighbour and asked him about the parrot. And when she heard her master's voice she said: "Take me home, O my uncle." So the man entered and took her from the thief's home.

8.

A society has been formed in one of the towns to combat illiteracy. This society has opened night-schools in the villages and towns to teach reading and writing to the peasants and artisans. One day it sent an inspector to a village carrying gifts as an encouragement to those learning in these night-schools. The peasants gathered around him, and the inspector called a woman from among them and asked her to read a word he indicated in a book in his hand. And she read in a loud voice: "Kerchief." He said to her: "Well done" and gave her a kerchief. Then he called forth a man and asked him to read a word at which he pointed. Hastily he read out: "Bull", but the word was something else. The inspector said to him: "Look well and read." And the man looked a second time and said: "Bull." Then his wife stood up and said: "My husband reads well but greatly needs a bull to plough the land."

9.

(Local News)

Jerusalem:- When Mr. F. went to (lit. approached) one of the windows of his house he saw that his car standing before the house had been jacked up in preparation for the removal of its tyres. He immediately informed the police-station and policemen rushed to the scene of the event. But they discovered no one in the vicinity of the car and investigation continues.

10.

Cairo:- (The Arab News Agency)

The Lebanese Aviation Company will begin operations at the end of this coming month, and has already bought thirteen commercial aircraft from Britain, and five aircraft from America for the transport of passengers between the Lebanon and the Arab countries. The Company will conclude agreements with American and British Aviation Companies for the conveyance of its passengers to Europe and America and back. And there are a number of Lebanese Aviation Companies who have obtained authorisation and are now busy obtaining the aircraft requested for them.

BIBLIOGRAPHY

The following short bibliography is suggested for those able to pursue the subject beyond the elementary level of this book:

1. القلقشندي [ʔal qalqaʃandii], صبح الأعشى [ṣubḥu l ʔaɛʃaa], Vols.I and II.

2. ابن النديم [ʔibnu l nadiimi], الفهرست [ʔal fahristu].

3. رسالة ابن الصائغ [risaalatu bni l ṣaaʔiɣi].

4. الأزهري [ʔal ʔazharii], وضاحة الأصول في الخط [waḍḍaaḥatu l ʔuṣuuli fii l xaṭṭi]

5. الأزهري [ʔal ʔazharii], تذكرة أولي الألباب في ما يتعلق بأسباب الكتابة وآلات الكتاب [taðkiratu ʔulii l ʔalbaabi fii maa yataɛallaqu bi ʔasbaabi l kitaabati wa ʔaalaati l kuttaabi].

6. مجلة مدرسة تحسين الخطوط الملكية [majallatu madrasati taḥsiini l xuṭuuṭi l malikiyyati] (Magazine of the Royal School of Calligraphy, Cairo).

7. محمد مؤنس [Muḥammad Muʔnis], الميزان المألوف في وضع الكلمات والحروف [ʔal miizaanu l maʔluufu fii waḍɛi l kalimaati wa l ḥuruufi].

8. محمد عزت [Muḥammad ɛizzat], خطوط عثمانية [xuṭuuṭun ɛuθmaaniyyatun] (for specimens of the different styles; Turkish text).